Organizations series

MW00333684

Series Editors: **Daniel King**, Nottingham Trent University and **Martin Parker**, University of Bristol

Organizations and Activism publishes books that explore how politics happens within and because of organizations, how activism is organized, and how activists change organizations.

Forthcoming in the series:

Reimagining Academic Activism:
Learning From Feminist Anti-Violence Activists
Ruth Weatherall

Guerrilla Democracy:
Digital-Activist Leadership for the 21st Century
Peter Bloom, Jamie Woodcock and **Owain Smolvic-Jones**

Sociocracy at Work:
Possibilities and Limitations of an Alternative Democratic Model of Organization
Martyn Griffin, Daniel King,
Ted Jennifer Rau and **Jerry Koch Gonzalez**

Studying Parties as Organizations:
Four Perspectives on Denmark's Alternative Party
Emil Husted

Find out more at

bristoluniversitypress.co.uk/organizations-and-activism

Organizations and Activism series

Series Editors: **Daniel King**, Nottingham Trent University and **Martin Parker**, University of Bristol

---

International advisory board:

Find out more at

bristoluniversitypress.co.uk/organizations-and-activism

ANARCHIST CYBERNETICS

Control and Communication in Radical Politics

Thomas Swann

BRISTOL
UNIVERSITY
PRESS

First published in Great Britain in 2021 by

Bristol University Press
University of Bristol
1-9 Old Park Hill
Bristol
BS2 8BB
UK
t: +44 (0)117 954 5940
e: bup-info@bristol.ac.uk

Details of international sales and distribution partners are available at bristoluniversitypress.co.uk

British Library Cataloguing in Publication Data
A catalogue record for this book is available from the British Library

ISBN 978-1-5292-0879-5 paperback
ISBN 978-1-5292-0878-8 hardcover
ISBN 978-1-5292-0881-8 ePub
ISBN 978-1-5292-0880-1 ePdf

Cover design: blu inc, Bristol
Front cover image: istock / leminuit

Bristol University Press uses environmentally responsible print partners.

Printed in Great Britain by CMP, Poole

Contents

About the Author

Thomas completed his PhD at the University of Leicester School of Management in September 2015. Prior to that, he studied social and political philosophy at Radboud University Nijmegen and philosophy at the University of Glasgow. Thomas is currently a Leverhulme Early Career Fellow in Politics and International Studies at Loughborough University. At Loughborough he is a member of the Anarchism Research Group and of the Anarchist Studies Network specialist group within the Political Studies Association.

Thomas's research examines the connections between anarchism and organisational cybernetics, focusing on radical and participatory approaches to democracy and intersectional anarchist political economy. In the past he has worked on a project led by Ruth Kinna and Alex Prichard looking at anarchist constitutional politics, and his recent work continues to sit broadly within this framework, examining the possibilities and challenges for anarchistic forms of social organisation.

Thomas is the co-editor of the collection *Anarchism, Organization and Management: Critical Perspectives for Students*, published in 2020 by Routledge.

Acknowledgements

First, I want to thank the editorial team at Bristol University Press with whom I have worked on publishing this book, Paul Stevens and Caroline Astley, as well as the series editors for including this in the 'Organizations and Activism' series, and Gordon Asher for his excellent work copy-editing this book. Second, my thanks go to my doctoral supervisors, Maria Puig de la Bellacasa and Stephen Dunne, my supervisors in my earlier studies, Benjamin Franks and Machiel Karskens, and to Ruth Kinna and Alex Prichard for including me in their work on anarchist constitutionalising. These relationships have shaped my thinking in different ways and this book would not be what it is now without them. I also want to thank my colleagues in the Anarchism Research Group at Loughborough University for giving me an unlikely home in academia and to the Leverhulme Trust for taking a chance on me and making possible the time needed to write this book. The friends and family who have helped me through the last decade are always in my thoughts and I know I wouldn't have been able to write this book without them. Finally, I must thank Janet for always being there for me and helping me steer through the roughest and calmest of waters. If cybernetics can be reduced to self-organised steering, then we are charting a course through life together, with Missy coming along for the ride.

Preface

Organizations and Activism

Series editors: Professor Daniel King, Nottingham Trent University, and Professor Martin Parker, University of Bristol

Organising is politics made durable. From co-operatives to corporations, Occupy to Facebook, states to NGOs, organisations shape our lives. They shape the possible futures of governance, policy making and social change, and hence are central to understanding how human beings can deal with the challenges that face us, whether that be pandemics, populism or climate change. This book series publishes texts that explore how politics happens within and because of organisations. We want to explore how activism is organised and how activists change organisations. We are also interested in the forms of resistance to activism, in the ways that powerful interests contest and reframe demands for change. These are questions of huge relevance to scholars in sociology, politics, geography, management and beyond, and are becoming ever more important as demands for impact and engagement change the way that academics imagine their work. They are also important to anyone who wants to understand more about the theory and practice of organising, not just the abstracted ideologies of capitalism taught in business schools.

Our books will offer critical examinations of organisations as sites of or targets for activism, and we will also assume that our authors, and hopefully our readers, are themselves agents of change. Titles may focus on specific industries or fields, or they may be arranged around particular themes or challenges. Our topics might include the alternative economy; surveillance, whistleblowing and human rights; digital politics; religious groups; social movements; NGOs; feminism and anarchist organisation; action research and co-production; activism and the neoliberal university; and any other subjects which are relevant and topical.

'Organizations and Activism' will also be a multidisciplinary series. Contributions from all and any relevant academic fields will be welcomed. The series will be international in outlook, and proposals from outside the English-speaking global North are particularly welcome.

This book, the first in our series, offers an exemplary and beautifully lucid contribution by bringing together the social movements of the early 21st century, the technologies of social media and virtual organising, and theories of anarchism and cybernetics. In *Anarchist Cybernetics: Control and Communication in Radical Politics* the Scottish activist and academic Thomas Swann applies theory and politics to contemporary examples, and wants us to think hard about self-organisation – that is to say, about forms of coordination that do not assume that human beings are too stupid to organise themselves. Whether party leaders, charismatic chiefs or a cadre of managers, we are often encouraged to believe that 'leadership' is required in order that human beings can assemble and do complicated things. This is an account of the insufficiency of ordinary people, and a justification for hierarchies of knowledge, status and reward.

These are vital issues at the present time, one in which many activists are reaching towards more local, horizontal and autonomous understandings of what a progressive politics might look like. The mechanisms of political party, nation state and multi-national corporation are in question, but there are real questions about how the small can be combined into something that scales up – that is to say, are capable of dealing with global challenges. To put it in more systemic terms, we need to understand whether and how large-scale coordination and communication can happen without central direction. Swann elegantly demonstrates how some classical forms of anarchism and contemporary ideas about networks can be combined to propose a future in which 'democracy' and 'participation' are words which refer to actual practices, not abstract concepts which have become clichés in the mouths of demagogues. Along the way, he demonstrates that anarchists are not against organisation, and that the small is beautiful and can also be very powerful.

We hope you enjoy this book, and if you want to discuss a proposal yourself, then email the series editors. We look forward to hearing from you.

2011: The Year ~~Everything~~ Nothing Changed

2011 was supposed to be the year when everything changed. Protests erupted across the planet, largely as a response to the worsening economic situation that followed the 2007–08 financial crash. These mobilisations, none of which seemed to have any real precedent in the years immediately prior to this post-crash emergence, were focused on challenging the political status quo. In more recent years, the tenets of these protest – rejecting the rule of governing elites, putting the concerns of the people at the forefront of politics and, of course, 'taking back control' – have become muddied by the rise of far-right populism. In 2011, however, the political challenge was not from the right but from a resurgent left, a left that had been positioned firmly on the sidelines of politics, at least since the peak of the alterglobalisation movement around the turn of the millennium if not since the fall of the Soviet Union a decade earlier. With respect to the economic realm, these movements brought class back into play, both as a defining feature of people's lives and of their dreams of a better future. 'We are the 99%' operated both as a slogan and as a framework that allowed people to express how common economic circumstances, like debt and precarity, impacted on their individual experiences. With respect to the political realm, this was echoed in scepticism, and at times outright rejection, of how societies were governed. In ostensibly democratic countries in North America and Europe, as much as in autocratic dictatorships in North Africa and the Middle East, protestors resented elite forms of governance that at best limited participation to ticking a box once every few years. This lack of accountability, they argued persuasively, was central to the problems that led not only to the financial woes brought on by the crash but also broader political and environmental crises.

The solution to this democratic deficit, and one of the orientations that separates the 2011 movements from the kind of far-right populism exemplified by Trump and Brexit, was to (re)instate democracy where it was lacking even in name and to deepen and expand it where it apparently already existed. Participation was at the heart of this. In different but connected ways, protest camps in Egypt, Madrid and New York, to name only the most prominent, demanded people be given a greater say in how their society and their lives are governed. For some, this meant checking the influence of corporations and other financial interests on political decision making, or instituting more representative means of electing members of parliaments and similar legislative bodies. For others, and in ways that were intimately connected with the structure and form of the camps in which they were assembled, democracy meant something entirely different to the representative form dominant around the world. Democracy, for them, involved a completely different system of participation and decision making. It was a mode of living with and relating to other people collectively, one that involved basing decisions on consensus as opposed to competition and giving everyone an active say in those matters that affected them. As protesters in Spain's Indignados movement put it, this was a call for ¡Democracia Real Ya!, for 'real democracy now!' Importantly, this was not simply a utopian dream, conjured up in response to dire economic and political circumstances, that no one had the first idea about how to enact. This vision of democracy, of participatory democracy, was something each of the camps around the world was putting into practice every day of their existence.

Across the world, ordinary people, many with little political experience, created open, public spaces at the heart of their towns and cities; spaces where they experimented with new and innovative ways of making direct and participatory democracy a reality. All of the major movements that rose up in 2011 – Occupy, the 15M movement and the Arab Spring – tried to use the spaces that they had carved out to create in the present, microcosms of the kind of futures they wanted to see come into being. In contexts of deepening economic recession, steep unemployment, rising debt and plummeting real wages, the camps were run based on the principle of mutual aid: people contributed what they were able to, whether that was resources, skills and abilities, or just time, and were free to take whatever they needed in terms of food and shelter. Camps were arenas of freedom of expression, with minorities and marginalised groups often feeling more able to live in ways they wanted to than they were able to in the societies that prevailed outside the camps. But perhaps one of the most important and enduring images of the camps involved their attempts to function as genuinely democratic communities. Occupy, in particular the original Occupy camp in the belly of the beast that is New York's financial district, Occupy Wall Street, has become synonymous with this manifestation of radical participatory democratic decision making. The core aspect of such practice involved all decision making being subject to approval by consensus. The general assembly, the sovereign body of the camp, was a space where anyone could speak and anyone could make a proposal for a decision to be taken. For a proposal to pass, it had to receive the consent of everyone present.

Of course, these miniature democratic communities did not last. By the end of 2011, little remained of these forms of real democracy that had been built in cities on almost every continent. The 15M encampments in Spain were evicted by the middle of that year. The Occupy movement in the United States saw their camps across the country evicted in a coordinated police action in the early hours of 15 November. In the months that followed, similar evictions took place in other countries, with Occupy London's camp at St Paul's Cathedral cleared in February 2012. While the Egyptian revolution initially led to a series of elections, in the years that followed the military took control, with the former Commander in Chief of the Armed Forces eventually becoming president in 2014. In Libya and Syria, the uprisings of 2011 morphed into bloody civil wars. Only Tunisia, of the countries rocked by protests during the Arab Spring, has made a transition to a representative, liberal democracy. Given these subsequent events, the explosion of participatory democracy in 2011 has resulted in little in the way of a direct realisation of these movements' goals. Indeed, instead of a more radically democratic world, we now live in one increasingly shaped by far-right populism.

The aim of this book is to help understand exactly how these experiments in participatory democracy operated and to identify the key functions of these forms of self-organisation, in the hope that they can be learned from in ways that might inform future movements' attempts to make participatory and more resilient the promise of real democracy.

The movement of the squares

While I draw here specific inspiration from Occupy, the 15M movement and the Arab Spring, focusing on how these movements were manifested in 2011, it is important to situate them within a wider wave of mobilisations across the world; what Paolo Gerbaudo (2017) has called 'the movement of the squares'. As Gerbaudo notes, these protests began with the self-immolation of Mohamed Bouazizi in Tunisia in December 2010, sparking the Arab Spring revolutions, with wider and longer-term influences that can be seen to have continued to at least the 2016 Nuit Debout protests of March 2016 in Paris, though these impacts could perhaps be extended further, to include both the 2019 protests in Hong Kong and the Climate Strike movement. Within this movement of the squares, Gerbaudo situates, in addition to those previously mentioned, mobilisations in Iceland, Greece, Turkey, Israel and Brazil, among other countries. What these have in common are both their origins – in various ways, responses to the financial crisis of 2008, the political crisis of (the absence of) democracy and the connections between these – and many of their methods – the occupation of public space, experimenting with forms of direct, participatory democracy and the creation of networks of mutual aid. Gerbaudo writes:

> This common culture has been epitomised by the ubiquity of the Guy Fawkes mask, borrowed from the blockbuster movie *V for Vendetta*, and by their use of a number of shared tactics, such as the use of social media as an organising platform, of protest camps, and of popular assemblies. Furthermore, protesters across all these counties have consistently expressed mutual solidarity by celebrating each other's victories, protesting against the repression of mobilisations abroad, by waving other movements' national flags in the squares, sending delegations to visit each other, and voicing the belief that their local mobilisations were the manifestations of a shared global struggle, or 'global revolution', against economic and political tyranny, and for real democracy. (Gerbaudo, 2017: 40–1)

Gerbaudo defines the politics of these movements as 'neo-anarchist'. I will return to the significance of the prefix 'neo' below. First, however, I want to consider the proposal that we might think of these movements, in particular Occupy, as 'anarchistic', if not explicitly anarchist. Mark Bray, in his book *Translating Anarchy* (2013), found that over a third of the key organisers of Occupy Wall Street identified as anarchist, with another third identifying as anarchistic in one way or another. Others have similarly recognised in Occupy an anarchist spirit, even if the camps themselves did not explicitly declare themselves as anarchist. In one FAQ, written by occupiers in New York, the response to the question '[w]ho are your leaders?' was: 'Occupy Wall Street is structured on anarchist organizing principles. This means there are no formal leaders and no formal hierarchy. Rather, the movement is full of people who lead by example. We are leader-full, and this makes us strong.'

The anarchism of Occupy, rather than flag-waving or sloganeering, is best exemplified by the form the movement took. Occupy was first and foremost a democratic movement, and this meant that any decisions taken in the camps had to be approved by one of two decision-making bodies: the general assembly and, later, the spokes-council. While decisions by the general assembly involved reaching consensus or near-consensus among all participants in the camp, the spokes-council aimed at making the process more efficient by involving only delegates from working groups and caucuses that were actively operating within the camp.

In different ways, similar organisational forms were witnessed across the movement of the squares, with participatory democracy a defining feature of these mobilisations. For Gerbaudo, the movement of the squares also highlighted the limitations of these forms of decision making, as they proved ineffective when it came to making decisions quickly and, importantly, to having a political impact beyond the camps themselves. The 'neo-anarchist' politics of the camps, he argues, involved a hybrid of anarchist organising and populism rooted in the idea of the nation or the people. Faced with the failure of anarchist forms of decision making, these movements tended to shift their terrain of struggle, from autonomous spaces of prefiguration that aimed to build a new world in the shell of the old, to an electoral politics where radical left populist parties aimed to achieve wide-ranging reform through the mechanisms and institutions of government rather than by engaging in direct action. In the final chapter of this book, I will return to this electoral turn in radical politics, but before doing so, an important point must be made in response to Gerbaudo's claim as to the failure of anarchism in the movement of the squares. While it is true that these movements and uprisings struggled with making mass participatory and democratic decision making a reality, it should also be remembered that these were by far the largest and most prolonged experiments in this form of politics thus seen, and as with any experiments, they provide lessons for learning and development to inform and shape future actions.

For Occupy in particular, the evolution that involved moving strategic decision making from the general assembly – marred by time-wasting and the involvement of those not active in the camps, including tourists attracted by the media – to the spokes-council marked a clear attempt to develop organisational processes in response to emerging challenges. More than anything else, the primary aim of this book is to illustrate in detail how a perspective taken from cybernetics and brought to anarchist organising can help show how these lessons from experience can be constructively heeded to inform future political organising. While the book is not intended as a *blueprint* for effective participatory and democratic organising, my hope is that, by exploring the functions of successful organisation, radical theory and practice can be advanced beyond the limitations of Occupy. This was something activists involved in Occupy were already grappling with when the movement was violently suppressed, and the argument presented in these pages can be read as a continuation of those attempts. Gerbaudo claims that the electoral turn attempted to 'marry the participatory ethos of the movement of the squares with a more strategic coordination of collective efforts' (2017: 245). Through an exploration of the potential application of anarchist cybernetics, I hope to show that these twin goals can both be realised through reinforcing, rather than abandoning, anarchist politics and the radically participatory and democratic forms of organisation that go with it. While '*neo*-anarchism' might aptly describe the melding of anarchist and populist politics, it need not suggest a necessary shift away from direct and participatory forms of democratic decision making.

Anarchist cybernetics

One of the central issues that motivates this book is how radically participatory and democratic forms of organisation can succeed where the 2011 protests failed. Undoubtedly, one aspect of addressing this, must involve the provision of explanations as to how movements like Occupy, the 15M movement or the Arab Spring might be able to mount a serious challenge to established political infrastructures and cultures. If an important factor in their failure had to do with an inability to ultimately resist the forces aligned against them – be this the repressive functions of the state, an established military apparatus, or entrenched economic interests – then starting to think about how radical movements can be successful must involve strategies for overcoming such forces and conditions. While this is a vital discussion for the radical left to undertake and for understanding how wide-reaching social change can be brought about, it is not the one this book aims to tackle. If the kind of alternatives that Occupy and other protests not only tried to articulate but actually tried to build are ever to succeed, as well as engaging in these discussions, these alternatives also need to be able to ensure that the fleeting glimpse of participatory democracy that they provided is actually sustainable. It is this question, of how the forms of democratic decision making that were experimented with in the 2011 protests can be maintained over time and, importantly, be practically effective in terms of making a form of organisation viable, that is the central concern of this book. To address this, and to provide a deep understanding of how effective and democratic organisation operates, the chapters that follow turn to two distinct but often overlapping political and academic traditions: anarchism and cybernetics.

That anarchism has a role to play in answering questions of how democratic organisation can function is perhaps unsurprising. The nature and role of democracy, as consistent with anarchist politics, has been a major topic of debates within anarchist circles, with discussion around whether democracy is a value, a means, method or process, an end, aim or objective, or indeed a combination of these. Nonetheless, anarchism has always been centrally concerned with self-organisation, with how groups of people can collectively govern themselves and make decisions about how they want to exist as a community. Anarchism emerged, as Ruth Kinna and Alex Prichard argue (2019), in the 19th century, from a critique of slavery and private property, and how both were made possible by the state. This involved identifying freedom as the absence of and resistance to domination, with democratic self-organisation playing a key role, though this specific terminology was not used at the time.

Bringing cybernetics into the discussion of how democratic organisation can function might seem less obvious. It may be that many people reading this are not aware of what exactly cybernetics is. The term conjures up exotic and fantastic images of cyborgs and cyberspace, of utopian dreams of automation, and dystopian terrors of uncontrollable artificial intelligence. While each of these conceptions certainly owes something to cybernetics, in general discourse it has tended to become simply a name, or more often a prefix, attached to anything that connotes some kind of technological advance. In fact, cybernetics emerged from the technological boom that followed the Second World War and at its inception concerned how any kind of system, be that an engineering or electronic system or a biological or social system, was organised; what the different parts of the system were, what function they played; and, importantly, how they operated together to make up the whole.

This book attempts to demonstrate that there is actually an intimate connection between anarchism and cybernetics. This connection, which has been recognised separately by different people involved in anarchist politics and the science of cybernetics, at different points in time, involves a recognition and understanding of a concept around which both traditions orbit, so to speak. This 'centre of gravity', as I will argue throughout the book and have already hinted at, is self-organisation. Cybernetics has been described as the science of effective organisation (Beer, 1974: 13). Effectiveness, it is argued, depends on an organisation's or system's ability to regulate itself in the face of challenges. For anarchism, self-organisation, as has already been mentioned, is a way of structuring decision making around the idea of non-domination; that individuals must be free and that such freedom requires collective organisation. This collective organisation in its turn requires processes of self-organisation, through which people come together to govern themselves. It has been suggested (Duda, 2013) that while these two traditions are both centrally concerned with self-organisation, they approach it in quite different ways: cybernetics from an interest in effectiveness, even efficiency; anarchism from the standpoint of social and political freedom. Something I want to explore in this book is how these stances actually represent two sides of the same coin. For figures in both traditions, self-organisation is at once the most effective way of organising society and the only way to ensure collective freedom or autonomy. The state, the bane of anarchism since its emergence, is attacked, for instance, not only because of the injustice and inequality it entails but as much because it is an ineffective way of organising social life. One of my main aims, then, is to show how these two orientations – practical effectiveness and political or moral desirability – overlap and point towards a shared approach to organisation.

Discovering cybernetics

Other than the rather sexy 'cyber' prefix or root, what many of the common assumptions about cybernetics share is that they all sit within the science fiction imagination, alongside connotations of high-technology, new frontiers of human consciousness and the meeting of biological bodies with mechanical, electronic and digital devices. These are associations you need to put to one side when reading this book. While cybernetics, as I will highlight, has intimate connections with robotics and the invention of the internet and related technologies, the word itself has a meaning that must be disentangled from such usages and associations. Importantly, the term cybernetics is not a recent invention, indeed it was not viewed as something new in the years following the Second World War, when the science of cybernetics emerged. Cybernetics' roots actually go as far back as the Ancient Athens of Plato, and it is in his dialogue *Alcibiades* that we find one of the first uses of the term, when Socrates notes the similarities between the art of governance and the steering of a ship (135a). The Ancient Greek word κυβερνήτης (rendered as kyvernítis, kyberné:te:s or kybernetes in modern Greek and in English) literally describes the act of piloting or steering. Ampère (1843) utilises the term, some 2,000 years later (in the French *cybernetique*), also to describe government, though as a science rather than an art. Etymologically, the word is also at work in the idea of a governor, both in terms of an individual who wields authority and a mechanical component that regulates speed.

In terms of the science of cybernetics that I am interested in here, it is the connotation of steering that is important. Like ships sailing towards a specific point on the horizon, systems, according to cybernetics, are goal-directed. Moreover, and again like ships, systems aim to achieve balance as they seek their goals. For ships, wind can blow them off course and they can correct for this through steering one way or the other. Systems, likewise, can be taken off course by changes in the environment around them and thus have to modify their behaviour to allow them to remain on course and achieve their goals. With respect to cybernetics, the steering that systems undergo is not conducted by an outside agency but by the system itself and its constituent parts. A simple contrast, to illustrate this difference, would be that between an automated toy car, programmed to avoid bumping into walls or falling off a surface, and a remote-controlled toy car controlled by the person playing with it. The former, through its utilisation of a series of sensors, can be said to be self-steering. The latter is steered externally. Cybernetics is concerned with the kinds of systems that steer themselves, that can be said to be self-organised and that are goal-directed.

My own discovery of cybernetics came about almost by accident. When I began my study for a PhD in a business school, one of the first tasks that was set as part of doctoral training was to write an essay on organisation theory, and having previously studied philosophy, specialising in anarchist political philosophy, I began reading about how key figures in the anarchist tradition had understood organisation. As well as exploring some of the classics, from authors such as Mikhail Bakunin and Peter Kropotkin, who feature throughout this book, I also looked into some of Colin Ward's work on anarchism and organisation. Ward is known for his work on housing and town planning, as well as his belief in anarchy as the condition that pertains when people are left to organise themselves without domination from institutions such as the state. For Ward, this meant making anarchism 'respectable'; not de-radicalising it, but attempting to have it taken seriously as a way in which society could be organised, and indeed, in many ways, actually is organised, underneath the domination and exploitation that anarchists are committed to fighting. In the mid-1960s, Ward wrote a short article called 'Anarchism as a Theory of Organization' (Ward, 1966). In it, he mentions cybernetics, noting that 'with its emphasis on self-organizing systems, and speculation about the ultimate social effects of automation, [cybernetics] leads in a similar revolutionary direction' as anarchism. This connection is echoed in a book by Dutch political theorist Marius de Geus (1989), one of the few authors to cover anarchism from an organisation theory perspective. Until recently, this work was only available in his native language. On Kropotkin's approach to organisation, de Geus writes (in an English translation of one chapter from his 1989 book):

> [Kropotkin's] vision of an anarchist society strongly resembles relatively modern bio-cybernetic organizational theories and systems of 'self-regulating' modules. In society there exist basic units (individuals, associations, communes, etc.) which have to possess autonomy, and which can co-operate and federate on a voluntary basis with the other units. (de Geus, 2014: 869)

The relationships between anarchism and cybernetics identified by Ward and de Geus – and, as I would discover when further exploring the topic, others, such as cybernetician Grey Walter and roboticist John McEwan – are based on an overlap around ideas of self-organisation and distributed control. One of the defining features of cybernetics is its focus on how systems can control themselves, without the need for an external controller to dictate their actions. Juxtaposed with an anarchist politics based on autonomy and collective organisation, the parallels are clear.

As I will discuss in Chapter 3, the organisational cybernetics of Stafford Beer is of particular interest in this regard. Not only does Beer highlight how cybernetics could be applied to social organisation, but connections can be drawn with radical politics, both through his involvement in Salvador Allende's socialist government in Chile in the early 1970s and through to how his work was taken up in the context of workers' cooperatives by Angela Espinosa, Roger Harnden, John Walker and others (for example, Walker, 2001; Espinosa et al., 2004; Espinosa and Harnden, 2007). Cybernetics shows us both how self-organisation operates in a technical sense and how political practices of self-organisation can be effective in responding to change and complexity. As such, it is in cybernetics that some of the answers to the questions raised by the failure of participatory democracy in Occupy and other movements might be found. What cybernetics provides us with is a set of tools that can be used to identify the key functions of effective self-organisation and, importantly, how these functions can be reproduced in the kind of non-hierarchical forms of organisation that anarchists are interested in building.

Overview of the book

In Chapter 2, I begin the discussion by providing an introduction to both anarchist organisation and the form of communication that is of interest here. Norbert Wiener subtitled the book that launched cybernetics (Wiener, 1961), 'control and communication in the animal and the machine'. While the focus here is on social organisation, and not on how cybernetics has been applied to biology or computers and other forms of engineering, this broad distinction between the two key areas of focus – control, on the one hand, and communication, on the other – serves to animate the structure of the argument of this book. In Chapter 2, this distinction is initially explored through an overview of anarchist organisation (control) and a corresponding model of interaction (communication). Anarchist organisation, it will be argued, is best understood as participatory and democratic, and as a method of self-organisation. Communication, in turn, will be framed as an issue of interaction in networks and of many-to-many communication, where broadcast hierarchies and centralisation of communication power are rejected.

Chapter 3 expands this introductory discussion by examining in more detail the connections between anarchism and cybernetics, focusing on a moment in 1963 when the overlap between the two traditions with respect to how self-organisation was understood occurred. Drawing in detail on an article published in the journal *Anarchy*, the chapter highlights the concept of *functional hierarchy* that animates both cybernetics and anarchist accounts of self-organisation. While recourse to a conceptualisation of hierarchy may seem at odds with anarchism's rejection of hierarchical domination, the chapter illustrates how a functional hierarchy in an organisation is in fact quite distinct from the structural hierarchies that anarchists are opposed to. A functional hierarchy helps define the roles different layers of organisation play and suggests how these layers can be open to democratic participation, in doing so, removing the hierarchy of some individuals or groups over others. The chapter uses the example of Occupy Wall Street to elaborate on this point and presents an anarchist version of Beer's Viable System Model.

Chapter 4, the first of two chapters that deal with control in anarchist cybernetics, explores these different levels of decision making in anarchist organisation, through the three-part distinction commonly made between tactics, strategy and grand strategy. This distinction makes it possible to identify the scope for autonomy in an organisation and where restrictions on autonomy may come into play. The freedom that parts of an organisation have to make tactical choices, it will be suggested, is limited in important ways by both overarching strategies and grand strategies, that respectively set out the goals and worldviews of the organisation. Through this discussion of strategy and grand strategy in anarchist cybernetics, the concept of prefiguration will be discussed as providing a way of thinking, about these functionally higher levels of decision making, that maintains the anarchist commitment to participation and democracy. Strategy, the chapter will show, must be understood as adaptable and experimental if it is to be meaningful in an anarchist cybernetic context.

Concluding the part of the book that covers the topic of control, Chapter 5 investigates the question of autonomy in anarchist cybernetics in more detail, articulating different definitions of autonomy at work in cybernetics and anarchism. For cyberneticians like Beer, autonomy was understood as distinct from how we use the word in everyday language: as a synonym for freedom and thus as a political ideal. Instead, in Beer's cybernetics, it is a *Functional Autonomy* that is at work, a concept that is concerned purely with the scope that different operational parts of an organisation have to make decisions with regard to their respective areas of responsibility. This autonomy is restricted by functionally higher levels of the organisation, which links to the previous chapter's discussion of strategic constraint. While, in anarchism, there are approaches to autonomy that value unrestrained freedom above all else, the chapter will focus on an account of *Collective Autonomy* that, like Beer's *Functional Autonomy*, is a freedom that exists with respect to collective organisation and that, as such, is constrained by the demands of that organisational context.

Chapter 6 opens the discussion of communication in the book by exploring exactly what is meant by the term in cybernetics and, through drawing on the related field of information theory, identifying the role effective communication plays in organisation. Central to this discussion is the idea of noise in a communication system. Typically, noise is considered as something that must be removed from a signal for it to be properly received and, from a cybernetic perspective, for that signal to be part of effective communication and organisation. Stepping away from this position, as it is captured in the Shannon-Weaver model of communication, the chapter draws on a range of arguments to suggest that noise can in fact play a constructive role in self-organisation, and as such, in anarchist cybernetics. Rather than presenting noise as a monolithic entity to be eliminated, through examining analysis conducted by activist-researchers involved in the Spanish 15M protests, it is argued that a specific form of noise, *pink noise*, should be present in systems of self-organisation.

In Chapter 7, the second chapter to focus on communication, the focus turns to how the kind of communication central to anarchist cybernetics and to self-organisation can be supported by technological infrastructures. Specifically, the chapter attempts to outline how social media platforms can facilitate interactive communication and participatory and democratic forms of organisation. Through discussing what it means for a social media platform to be an alternative and by responding to some of the key critiques of mainstream social media, it is argued that an effective platform for anarchist self-organisation needs to include a range of functions. Avoiding overly technical accounts of how digital platforms are constructed, the chapter highlights the communication and organisational mechanisms that would allow an alternative social media platform to enable self-organisation as it has been discussed throughout the book; such as tools to collectively manage autonomy and strategy, as well as effective communication.

Chapter 8 draws the book to a conclusion by returning to the questions raised by the 2011 uprisings, with a focus on how radical politics has developed in the years since. Across the world, as the movement of the squares came to an end, much of the radicalism it had helped give form to redirected itself towards an unlikely terrain: electoral politics. In the US and UK, much of the political outrage following the financial crash has found its way into support for the traditional centre-left political parties: the Democratic Party in the US, in the form of Bernie Sanders' campaign for the presidential nominations in

2016 and 2020; the Labour Party in the UK, with Jeremy Corbyn's election as leader in 2015. In Spain and Greece, Podemos and Syriza respectively rose to prominence and in both cases (very recently for Podemos in its new form) held power. This final chapter considers this electoral turn and whether there is a place within it for the kind of self-organisation seen in the general assemblies of Occupy and other movements. It concludes by suggesting that a populist and hegemonic anarchism may have a role to play and that self-organisation can yet be a mobilising force for the radical left.

2

Radical Left Organisation and Networks of Communication

Before defining and exploring what a meeting of anarchism and cybernetics might mean for radical politics, I need to first elaborate on the two central areas of interest of this book: organisation and communication. As mentioned in the previous chapter, Norbert Wiener (1961) defined cybernetics as the science of control and communication. As Chapter 3 will make clear, control, in this context, does not refer to top-down command but to a more horizontal process of self-organisation. As such, in this chapter, I will explore the question of control in anarchism by discussing how anarchism has developed as a theory of organisation and what this means for participatory and democratic structures of decision making in practice. For anarchism, organisation entails creating effective political structures that preserve both the autonomy of individuals and that of the different parts that constitute the organisational whole. Importantly, this is an attempt to respond to an anarchist analysis of the ills of society, which are understood as resulting from capitalist economic exploitation and centralised, authoritarian domination. Communication comes into this picture in so far as organisation and decision making within it necessitates platforms by means of which individuals and groups can share information and collectively shape the world around them. As I will highlight, horizontal, networked forms of communication, in which everyone can communicate with everyone else, are considered a necessary condition for the effectiveness of anarchist organisation. Over the last three decades, internet and digital media, such as social media platforms, have been increasingly linked to this conception of organisation and communication and will play a key role in how they are examined in this chapter and throughout the rest of this book.

Anarchism as a theory of organisation

The vision of anarchism predominant in the public imagination is often one of disorder and chaos. In Joseph Conrad's *The Secret Agent*, the anarchist is depicted as a bomb-throwing assassin, a provocateur acting in the name of terror and mayhem. Across the mainstream political spectrum, it is common to see individuals being labelled as anarchists if they are seen to be disregarding appropriate behaviour, perhaps with a view to personal gain above all else. However, as I discussed in the introduction, the reality is that anarchism has, from its inception, insisted that the anarchy that is desired and which anarchists work to create is synonymous with order, rather than chaos. Anarchism, as its theorists and activists from the middle of the 19th century onwards have argued, is a theory of organisation, not turmoil. Pierre-Joseph Proudhon (1840), the first person to self-identify positively as an anarchist, wrote that 'society finds its highest perfection in the union of order with anarchy'. Far from the mainstream image of anarchists as the unprincipled agents of disaster, anarchism represents a theorisation of how society can be structured to enable liberty and solidarity, a society based on the principle of mutual aid, where the needs of all are met through cooperation and the sharing of resources. As anarchist studies scholar Ruth Kinna puts it, 'anarchism is a doctrine that aims at the liberation of peoples from political domination and economic exploitation by the encouragement of direct or non-governmental action' (2005: 1). For anarchism, then, the way this society can be achieved is the creation and development of forms of organisation that put people in control of their own lives and of the decisions that impact on them.

Over almost the last two centuries, anarchists have resisted and sought to replace a range of structures that are implicated in the kind of domination and exploitation they wish to see end, including, but not limited to; capitalism, the state, organised religion, monarchy, patriarchy, racism and colonialism, homophobia and, in recent decades, transphobia, ecological destruction and the exploitation of animals. In anarchist theory, there is a direct connection drawn between the sources of these systems of oppression and the actions that need to be taken to liberate people from them. Others in the broad socialist tradition, such as some strands of Marxism, have pinpointed systems of economic exploitation as the primary site of the struggle for freedom, and in doing so have disregarded the specific role of broader systems of hierarchical domination in the subjugations that people experience. This has led some sections of the wider socialist movement to propose and even enact authoritarian and totalitarian systems of government as part of programmes aimed at lessening or eliminating economic exploitation. Anarchists have, on the other hand, in a range of different ways, proposed that how society is governed is at least as important as how economic resources are managed. Instead of aiming to construct structures of political domination to end economic exploitation, anarchism contends that how society should be structured must reflect the need for both economic and political liberation, an end to not only economic misery and alienation but also political control from above. As Kinna notes, in the passage quoted previously, the means of anarchism involves direct and non-government action.

Anarchist philosopher Benjamin Franks defines this kind of direct action in the anarchist tradition as action that 'refers to practical prefigurative activity carried out by subjugated groups in order to lessen or vanquish their own oppression' (2006: 115). Direct action, as a method of anarchism, involves those who are exploited and dominated acting for themselves, to change their situations in ways that do not depend on the goodwill or charity of others. Only by people taking control of their own lives, collectively, rather than as individuals, can a society be created in which no one is exploited or dominated. This change cannot come, it is argued, through a government that rules over people, or be brought about by the benevolence of a class whose wealth is dependent on the exploitation of people, animals and the environment. Central to this idea of direct action is the concept of prefiguration. I will return to this notion of prefiguration in Chapter 4. For the moment, with respect to defining anarchism as a theory of organisation, it should be noted that prefiguration refers to the means or methods of political action mirroring its ends or goals and thus reflecting the values that underpin them. For anarchism, the aim of politics is a world free of domination and exploitation. To achieve this, methods must be used that actually enact these principles in the present. In other words, we should aim for the organisations that we build today to themselves be as free of domination and exploitation as the world we want to create in the future. By acting prefiguratively, then, the utopian future is brought into existence, to the greatest extent possible, in the here and now. As such, a central reason for prefiguration's importance for anarchism is that it shapes how anarchists organise.

This prefigurative spirit of anarchist politics is one of its defining characteristics, especially so when it comes to questions of anarchist organisation. From the outset anarchism came into conflict with state-centred approaches to socialism and communism. Marx himself feuded publicly with Proudhon and with Mikhail Bakunin, who became one of the leading figures as anarchism acted as a strong pole of attraction in the growing revolutionary movements of the 19th century. In the International Workingmen's Association (IWA), which represented the first major attempt at uniting anti-capitalist currents under a single banner and strategy, anarchists, such as those clustered around the Swiss Jura Federation, rejected Marx's commitment to taking control of the state as a central plank of revolutionary strategy. For the anarchists in the International (as the IWA was known) – also referred to as the First International to distinguish it from the Second and Third Internationals that followed it in the 20th century – the state represented the key form of centralised and hierarchical political domination. While the Marxists saw the state as a potentially positive force that could bring about an end to economic exploitation, the anarchists challenged this, arguing that the actions of the state, whether controlled by capitalists or by socialist revolutionaries, would inevitably create forms of authoritarian domination. The centralisation of political authority was an essential feature of the state, something that could not be separated from its very existence. History, it seems, has proved the anarchists right. The Soviet Union, representing a capture of the power of the state by socialists, led not to economic and political freedom but to totalitarianism and torment.

Anarchism's rejection of political centralisation and hierarchy applied not only to the desired form of a socialist society, but also to the organisations that could be used to bring such a society about. While those who followed Marx in the First International argued for the development of political parties who would, either through revolution or election, seize state power, the anarchists championed the building of organisations that were prefigurative, insofar as they aimed at creating the conditions of the future society in the present. Principally, these were organisations that embodied anti-capitalism through the enactment of mutual aid and anti-domination, through participatory and democratic decision-making structures. It is these forms of anarchist organisation that are capable of realising the kind of 'order' which Proudhon wrote about. As I will argue throughout this book, effective regulation of society comes not through top-down domination but through a form of control embedded in self-organisation and in democratic participation. In the alterglobalisation movement that arose in the 1990s, and later in the uprisings of 2011, it was horizontal and participatory organisation that came to the fore. In practice, this has been articulated in different and contextualised ways, ranging from clandestine underground cells, made necessary in situations where political activity is criminalised, to the 'vanguard' anarchism of platformist tendencies (Franks, 2006: 227–30), to the kind of networked organisation that is perhaps more in keeping with the commitment to autonomy and self-organisation that I have been discussing (Ward, 1973: 51–2; Gordon, 2008: 14–17; Graham, 2011).

Of this networked form of anarchist organisation, Franks writes:

> In a network, if a particular activity is considered by a participant to be inappropriate they are free either to abstain or even undertake opposing action outside of the network. It would still be possible for them to rejoin in other events that did meet their interests. This method of organisation has prefigurative elements favourable to anarchists. It employs a free contract and allows for greater flexibility of operation. (Franks, 2006: 225–6)

As well as providing participatory forms of decision making in which everyone is able to play a role in making decisions that affect them, such a network, of the type Franks describes and to which I will return to later in this chapter, allows for a level of voluntarism in anarchist organisation that protects individuals and minorities from being forced to comply with decisions of a majority. For Colin Ward (1973) voluntary participation is one of the defining features of anarchist organisation, and a pillar of the tradition has been the belief that those wishing to part from a collective entity should face no hardship for choosing to do so and that those wishing to join should face no barriers. This, of course, creates a tension in anarchist organising between the autonomy of the parts and the effectiveness of the whole; a tension managed in a range of different ways by anarchist organisations, with varying degrees of success. In Chapter 5, I discuss consensus decision making, which is one of the processes often used to help negotiate this tension.

One of the forms of organisation that anarchists have proposed is the federation. Proudhon, writing in the earliest days of the anarchist tradition, proposed federalism as a form of governance that both allowed different groupings to come together and negotiate their coexistence and provided a way to manage the conflict between authority and autonomy (Prichard, 2012). While there are different forms of federalism advocated by anarchism and other forms of organisational theory and practice, the concept generally refers to a mode of organisation, applied to revolutionary groups or society as a whole, whereby separate parts are brought together within a decision-making body created to govern common areas of concern. Each of the parts of the federation will send delegates or representatives to this higher body, a council or parliament of sorts, that will make such decisions. The contributions of the delegates to the decision making is based on the mandate they have been given by those they represent. Often, the various parts of the federation will have some level of autonomy in their own decision making, with respect to decisions concerning areas that are not of concern to other parts of the federation. For instance, different neighbourhoods in a city might have control over how a resource such as housing is managed in their respective areas, but recycling or waste disposal could be a matter concerning a group of neighbourhoods and so they would federate together to create a level of decision making running across each of the neighbourhoods. In turn, something like water treatment might be a concern for a whole city and so a series of cross-neighbourhood decision-making bodies could again federate together to create a level of decision making for the city as a whole. Federalism describes this approach to governance, where different layers of decision making, from those of the smallest community to those at a regional or even global level, are nested on top of one another, with some method of democratic participation provided for at each level – for example, delegates or representatives being mandated to make decisions at the level above, on behalf of others at the level below.

Federalism, therefore, is seen by anarchists and others as a means of providing for decision making at scales beyond the immediate communities people live in, that maintains a level of autonomy for those communities. Indeed, Bakunin (1871), for example, writes the following of an anarchist vision of society: '[t]he future social organization should be carried out from the bottom up, by the free association or federation of workers, starting with the associations, then going on to the communes, the regions, the nations, and, finally, culminating in a great international and universal federation.' Elsewhere (1866), he similarly argues that '*all organizations must proceed by way of federation from the base to the summit, from the commune to the coordinating association of the country or nation*'. In federalism, then, we have a vision of organisation in which smaller local organisations, free associations or cooperatives, link up with one another at the level of the commune. Communes then link up with one another at the level of regional council, and so on, level by level, until we reach the level of an international council. With respect to decisions outside the remit of higher-level bodies, the individual units at lower levels are able to act autonomously. As I will discuss throughout this book, while this restricts the autonomy of the parts – by subjecting them to the decisions of higher levels in the federation – this is consistent with the commitment to democracy as these restrictions are produced in participatory and democratic ways. For Proudhon, Bakunin and many others, federalism is a way of reconciling the respect for autonomy with the need for cohesive political organisation from the local to the global.

Self-organisation and democracy

As I will explore in the next chapter, self-organisation is one of the core concepts at work in discussions of cybernetics. It is also of vital importance for anarchist theories of organisation. In the context of anarchist and radical social movement organisation, self-organisation refers to processes that are participatory and democratic and through which people come together in a collective to produce an organisational form with capabilities beyond those of its individual parts. Self-organisation does not require top-down control, but instead involves the kind of decision-making processes that have always been part of the anarchist tradition and that allow for groups to develop goals and achieve them through collective discussion and cooperation. In self-organisation, it is also crucial that each of the parts of the organisation – individual people or sub-groupings – retain a level of autonomy, in a similar manner to how federations operate. Alexander Galloway writes that in self-organisation, 'each agent is endowed with the power of local decision according to the variables and functions within its own local scope' (2014: 114; see also Escobar, 2009). John Duda similarly argues that self-organisation can be understood as 'radical democracy and horizontal self-determination' (2013: 57; for a thorough historical overview of self-organisation in both anarchism and cybernetics, see Duda's unpublished doctoral thesis, 2012). Put simply, self-organisation can be defined as a situation where people *organise themselves* through processes of collective decision making. A pivotal question for anarchist organisation, is the extent to which self-organisation can be accurately described as democratic. In the chapter thus far, I have defined anarchist organisation in terms of participatory democracy. It ought to be recognised, however, that this link between anarchism and democracy is not an unproblematic one.

As Gordon (2016) notes, the positive connection between anarchism and democracy is a relatively recent phenomenon. Democracy was considered by early anarchists, such as Proudhon and Bakunin, as a term that solely referred to institutional representative democracy, with elections as a means of selecting a set of governing individuals. The form of collectively organising society these anarchists championed was not referred to as 'democratic' at the time. As Malatesta put it,

> [e]ven in the most democratic of democracies it is always a small minority that rules and imposes its will and interests by force [...] Therefore, those who really want 'government of the people' in the sense that each can assert his or her own will, ideas and needs, must ensure that no one, majority or minority, can rule over others [...] (Malatesta, quoted in Gordon, 2016)

Markus Lundström (2020) argues that the anarchist rejection of democracy is based on the identification of democracy as a system of state governance and as such an identification with illegitimate authority. A state governed democratically, in the interests of the majority, remains a state and thus the relations of domination that inevitably exist between the state and its subjects endure. If a majority support a particular configuration of state government, by voting for political parties or representatives, they are supporting domination of the minority as well as domination of themselves in so far as they are opting to be governed by a separate group such as those who sit in parliament. For anarchists, then, whether democratic (in the majoritarian sense) or not, the state is a dominating force.

Particularly through engagement with Murray Bookchin's work from the 1970s onwards, however, the term 'democracy' has been appropriated by many anarchists as a way of describing the governance structures and processes they want to build for a world that involves a rejection of the state. Gordon (2016) writes that '[t]rue democracy, in this account, can only be local, direct, participatory, and deliberative, and is ultimately achievable only in a stateless and classless society'. True or real democracy is contrasted here with the false democracy of representative systems of government. While the arguments of Gordon and others are important – particularly with respect to concepts of democracy that have fundamental links to colonialism and neocolonialism, as a legacy of the European Enlightenment – I will retain the use of the term throughout this book, but use it to refer to participatory democracy rather than representative forms of government that involve elections. In doing so I take inspiration from the Zapatistas and the Kurdish liberation movement, in Chiapas and Rojava respectively, where, Gordon recognises, the inheritance of democracy is not that of settler colonialism. Democracy can refer to something far more fundamental than representative forms of (state-based and therefore dominating) government. While Gordon critiques Cindy Milstein's (2010) recourse to Lincoln's dictum that democracy is government by the people, for the people and of the people, this seems a particularly apt way of framing anarchist processes of governance and self-organisation, and surely the guilt by association with a figure revered for his representative democratic credentials can be overcome. Whatever the understandable qualms as to its use and associations, I would suggest that we can constructively choose to use the word 'democracy' to describe the kind of decision-making structures anarchists are in favour of. Ultimately, this may well be a question of semantics rather than one concerning the content of concepts and their realisation in political practice (if one objects to the use of 'democracy' in this book, perhaps imagining another word in its place when it appears will suffice).

Intersectional anarchism

In this book, the focus throughout will be on the structure and the functionality of anarchist organisation and the communication practices and infrastructures that support it. While these provide channels through which anarchist approaches to questions of power and structural inequality can be realised and developed, this side of anarchist politics will not be explored in detail here. That being said, it is important to recognise some of the recent advances in anarchist thought and consider briefly how they relate to organisation. Over the last decade or so, much of anarchist politics, both theory and practice, has become infused with insights from intersectionality. Intersectionality was a term coined by legal theorist Kimberlé Crenshaw (1989) in the late 1980s (although it has precedent roots in the works of, for example, the Combahee River Collective, 1979, Hazel Carby, 1982 and bell hooks, 1981) to describe the way multiple different lines of oppression 'intersect' with one another to produce specific configurations of oppression acting on different individual people and groups. For Crenshaw and other early theorists of intersectionality, the aim was to develop an understanding of how women of colour faced different conditions to white women. This was a response to and evolution of the dominant strands of feminist thought, at the time, which tended to view women as a single category. Intersectionality illustrated that as well as oppression along gender lines, women of colour also faced oppression along racial lines, meaning that a homogeneous feminism would not be able to respond to the problems they faced. This approach was extended to cover class as well – for example, working-class women would face different forms of oppression from middle- or upper-class women – and later to a wider range of intersecting axes of oppression, through what has come to be called the 'matrix of domination' (Hill Collins, 2000).

Intersectionality has its roots in radical politics, with one of its first articulations coming from the Combahee River Collective, a group of black feminist activists:

> We are actively committed to struggling against racial, sexual, heterosexual, class oppression, and see as our particular task the development of integrated analysis and practice based upon the fact that the major systems of oppression are interlocking. The synthesis of these oppressions creates the conditions of our lives... We believe that sexual politics under patriarchy is as pervasive in black women's lives as are the politics of class and race. We also often find it difficult to separate race from class from sex oppression because in our lives they are most often experienced simultaneously. (Combahee River Collective, 1979)

These insights have been taken up in a range of different ways across the spectrum of radical politics. Anarchism has been no exception, with activists and theorists applying the insights of intersectionality to their own politics, as well as further expanding and developing intersectionality theory itself, by bringing to it a focus on the state as another source of domination that works alongside previously acknowledged systems of domination, such as patriarchy, white supremacy and capitalism (for example, Price, 2007; Volcano and Rogue, 2012; Lazar, 2015). For anarchists that have taken on board what intersectionality theory has to say about oppression and exploitation, it is the structural conditions of these integrated systems of domination that are the focus. Echoing pioneers of intersectionality, such as the Combahee River Collective and bell hooks, intersectional anarchists reject the liberal tendency to focus on oppression as an issue of prejudice or bias, and instead focus on the historical structures that shape people's lives and that serve to produce and reinforce oppressive conditions in ways that go far beyond the oppressive behaviour of particular individuals (for an overview see Kinna, 2019: 157–64).

One framing that illustrates this approach, is the contrast drawn by anarchists between the idea of 'classism' and the structural forms of economic exploitation that they are determined to resist. Shannon and Rogue, for example, argue:

> While we believe that class elitism exists, often this opposition to 'classism' does not recognize the unique qualities of capitalism and can lead to a position that essentially argues for an end to class elitism under capitalism. As anarchists, we do not just oppose class elitism, we oppose class society itself. We do not want the ruling class to treat us nicer under a system based on inequality and exploitation (i.e. capitalism). We want to smash capitalism to pieces and build a new society in which classes no longer exist – that is, we fight for socialism. Anarchists, as part of the socialist movement, are well-placed to critique this liberal interpretation of intersectionality. (Shannon and Rogue, 2009: 7)

Rather than aiming to addresses prejudice against working-class people through, for instance, smashing the so-called 'class ceiling' and seeing more working-class people employed in senior corporate roles, anarchism is directed against the system of capitalism that, however it may be reformed, will always be dependent on an exploited class of workers and a exploitative class of employers and owners of property. Seeing some working-class people join the ranks of the employers by being promoted to sit on corporate boards does nothing, so the argument goes, to address the structural exploitation that is capitalism. bell hooks makes a similar point, concerning the challenging of racism, when this is understood as merely a problem of individual behaviour: 'That's just another bullshit way of people not wanting to name the power and institutionalized strength of white supremacy. We all may have prejudices, but we're not all part of a system that reinforces, reinvents and reaffirms itself every day of our lives, systemically' (hooks and Lowens, 2011).

While anarchism has much to learn from intersectionality theory – which in part involves finding ways to better articulate sentiments that already exist in the anarchist tradition, in, for instance, the work of figures such as Emma Goldman, Voltairine de Cleyre and Lucy Parsons – anarchism, in its turn, also potentially has something to offer intersectional theory, through its identification of the state as a central component of the matrix of oppression and exploitation. Francis Dupuis-Déri, for example, argues for extending hooks' (2000) formulation of 'imperialist white-supremacist capitalist patriarchy' to include the state: 'while discussing the matrix of domination and intersectionality, it is possible to refer to "capitalism, sexism, racism, statism" as well as to "class, sex, race, and state"' (2016: 54). Rather than the state playing an ancillary, supporting role in relation to different lines of domination and exploitation, Dupuis-Déri contends that the domination emanating from the state has its own logic and that, at times, its operation is more prominent that other aspects or forms of oppression. State domination, he writes, operates at three levels: (1) the macro or systematic level of 'a system that imposes its dynamic on a population and a territory over which it claims to exercise "sovereignty"'; (2) the meso or institutional level of 'a large number of institutions, including parliament, government departments, and the courts [...] but also state companies (often monopolistic) and public services, such as public schools'; and (3) the micro or individual level of a dominant class of people that 'includes a variety of members with different statuses, degrees of power, and material, psychological, and symbolic privileges' (Dupuis-Déri, 2016: 44–9).

Organisationally, taking an intersectional approach to anarchist politics wedded to the prefigurative commitments of much contemporary anarchist activism, the structures that anarchists build in the present, ought to aim at realising a world in which the matrix of domination, understood as incorporating the centralised power of the state, is eliminated. A pivotal focus, then, is finding ways of creating relationships between individuals and groups that are not characterised by hierarchy, domination and exploitation, be that based on gender, class, race or authoritarianism, or indeed other factors intersectional and anarchist theories have highlighted, including, for instance, heteronormativity and ableism. In this book, I focus on how organisational structures can be realised that aim to do away with the kind of domination that we see in how the state and other centralised, hierarchical institutions, such as political parties and mainstream trade unions, operate. The aim here, therefore, is not to directly address the ways in which patriarchy, white supremacy or capitalism are realised and reinforced in forms of organisation. Which is not to say that some of the mechanisms discussed here, such as consensus decision making, cannot also be used to address these systematic oppressions and exploitations. The central focus here, however, is on how *political* domination can be resisted, through the realisation of alternative forms of organising. Theorising an organisational response to the matrix of domination as a whole will need to be taken up elsewhere.

Social media, communication and networks

With respect to both the alterglobalisation movement and the uprisings of 2011, the use of the internet, latterly alongside social media, has often been picked out as a defining feature of these new waves of anarchist and radical mobilisation. An activist quoted in Paul Mason's book *Why It's Kicking Off Everywhere* commented of the Arab Spring revolutions that they were 'planned on Facebook, organized on Twitter and broadcast to the world via YouTube' (Mason, 2011: 14). At the time, much was made of how social media platforms such as Facebook and Twitter were enabling activists to organise in environments that heavily restricted political organising, and to do so in ways that made fast, responsive and non-hierarchical organisation more effective than it had ever been in the past. Jeffrey Juris (2005: 191; see also 2008, 2012), for instance, argues that '[b]y significantly enhancing the speed, flexibility and global reach of information flows, allowing for communication at a distance in real time, digital networks provide the technological infrastructure for the emergence of contemporary network-based social movement forms.' Leah Lievrouw echoes this point: 'networked communication technologies have allowed movements to shift from relatively centralized, hierarchical organizational structures to highly decentralized, loosely affiliated contingent networks that link a wide variety of groups, actors, and interests without imposing a single dominant agenda or program of action' (Lievrouw, 2011: 175).

The riots that took place in London in August 2011 articulate very well the potential that social media holds for radical forms of self-organisation. While the riots – a response by heavily policed working-class young people, largely young people of colour, to the death of Mark Duggan in a police shooting – are not commonly framed as part of the 'movements of the squares' uprisings of 2011, they nonetheless contain similar hallmarks when it comes to how social media was being utilised to support new ways of organising.

At the time, BlackBerry mobile phones were available on low-cost contracts, from as little as £5 a month. While BlackBerry devices are now aimed primarily at businesses, in 2011 they were ubiquitous and were almost synonymous with mobile computing, in the way the iPhone is today. Rather than the phones themselves being of interest during the riots, it was the standard messaging application that was viewed as being influential in how the riots were organised. First, BlackBerry Messenger allowed users to send messages to lists of contacts at no cost, providing those contacts were also using the app. This provides an example of the formation of a networked communication infrastructure. Second, thanks to the BlackBerry's security focus, this communication network was impossible to hack into (as even at that time, Research in Motion, the company that made the phone, was appealing the market of business and government use). The strong encryption of the Messenger app meant that the police were unable to monitor the communications platform that was being used to organise the riots. It is also important to consider what 'organisation' meant in the context of the riots. Of course this was not a formal organisation or even a fluid one with shifting membership like a social movement. The riots, however, were organised in the sense that any social phenomenon is organised and bound by certain formal or informal processes and rules. In attempting to understand how this organisation came about in the case of the riots, a consideration of how a system or network analysis explains how a crowd is organised is useful: a series of parts (individual rioters) were connected through a communication network (via BlackBerry Messenger) that enabled them to respond to what was happening in real time and in doing so to operate as a semi-coherent whole. For the rioters, this involved being able to share information about police locations and safe routes through the city (Fuchs, 2012).

For theorists engaged in analysing both events like the riots and more formal social movement mobilisations, these newly prevalent communication technologies led to a focus on the self-organising properties of swarms and networks. While 'network' has become a buzzword in the last decade or so, it is far from being a new concept, and the terminology of 'networks' is present across a range of political thinking and writing, rather than it being a concept restricted to radical, left-wing political analyses. Manuel Castells, one of the authors most closely associated with network theory, defines networks in terms of flows of information and resources between interconnected nodes. In networks, it is argued, the flows, the lines of connection, are more important in terms of analysis than what is traveling along them. Castells (1996: 469) describes this dynamic as 'the power of flows over flows of power'. This idea of a network goes back at least to the early 1960s and the work of Paul Baran (1962) and the RAND Corporation in developing communication systems that could withstand a nuclear attack. In such an event, a centralised command and control structure would be vulnerable to the centre being rendered inoperable, thus eliminating the possibility of communication with other parts of the system. A decentralised or distributed network structure, on the other hand, with either multiple centres or no centre at all, would be more resilient. If one part was destroyed, the other parts could continue to communicate with one another. This approach to communication paved the way for the internet, itself originally developed with military functions in mind.

Networks have also been observed in the case of non-human systems. Slime mould, a cluster of single-celled organisms, functions much in the same way a network does. Individual cells receive and transmit information about their environment through the network, allowing it to function almost as a single body. If one cell in the network recognises a good source of food, this information will be passed from cell to cell and the network as a whole will extend itself towards that source of food. In search of food, then, the slime mould network, despite lacking both a nervous system and a brain, operates as a single, unified whole. Networks that function as human social systems are considered to work in similar ways, with coherent, purposeful behaviour being made possible through the communications and subsequent actions of the network form, without the need for central control functions. Interestingly, slime mould has been shown to effectively replicate human transport networks. In experiments where food sources have been placed at locations on a map and in quantities designed to represent the population density of towns and cities, slime mould networks extend across the map in ways that often mirror train or road networks (for example, Tero, et al., 2010). A similar example of the functioning of a non-human network is that of a flock of birds. Mitchel Resnick describes the behaviour of a flock as follows:

> Each bird in the flock follows a set of simple rules, reacting to the movements of the birds nearby it. Orderly flock patterns arise from these simple, local interactions. None of the birds has a sense of the overall flock pattern. The bird in front is not a leader in any meaningful sense – it just happens to end up there. (Resnick, 1996: 2)

These understandings of networks and swarms, where a collection of parts – be it slime mould cells, birds or people – operate as a purposeful whole, are also linked to developments in communication technology. Indeed, the early work on networks at the RAND Corporation was focused on technology that would support the kind of network that could continue to function in the event of a nuclear attack. For theorists like Castells (see also Rheingold, 2003; Hardt and Negri, 2004), what has been of interest in recent years is how internet and other information communication technologies have become common in everyday life;

and how in doing so they have facilitated the kind of networked forms of organisation that, in relation to social movements, enable non-hierarchical decision making. One of the founders of Twitter, for instance, made direct reference to the example of the flock of birds, using this to describe the social media platform: '[i]t is something that looks incredibly choreographed and complicated but it is rudimentary behaviour among individuals in "real time" that allows them to behave as though they were a single organism' (quoted in Baker, 2011: 2.7). As Howard Rheingold (2003) notes, the new technologies, that have been available from the end of the 20th century – including internet features such as listservs and forums and then later social media platforms – heightened network dynamics and favoured a specific form of communication: '[m]obile and deskbound media such as blogs, listservs and social networking sites allow for many-to-many communication.'

Many-to-many communication

This concept – many-to-many communication – is one that perhaps best sums up how social media and networked communications operate. One of the first instances of the term being used is by psychiatrist Jurgen Ruesch. Ruesch does not go into detail on the topic, but in an essay published in 1957 identifies four forms of human communication: one-to-one, one-to-many, many-to-one and many-to-many (Ruesch, 1957, see also Ruesch and Bateson, 1968: 39–40). One-to-one communication refers to what we experience in a conversation with one other person, either in person or mediated by technology. In this situation, the signal and the message are transmitted between two points, the sender and the receiver, the speaker and the listener. One-to-many communication covers the kind of situation found in typical broadcast communication, where a signal is transmitted from a central point and received by an audience of multiple people, for example in the context of radio or television broadcasting or the case of print media. Many-to-one communication covers situations such as government consultations, where a central point or individual receives information from a multitude of sources; for instance, a government department might request the population's thoughts on a particular policy and provide a platform, either online or perhaps through a form that can be completed and returned by post, to facilitate the relevant messages being transmitted and received. Many-to-many communication, in contrast, involves the type of communication commonly found in decentralised or distributed networks, where multiple nodes can send messages to one another without a central point of convergence.

More recently, many-to-many communication has been defined in response to the question 'who gets to say something to how many?'. Drawing on Jensen and Helles (2011: 519–20; see also McQuail, 2010: 144) and in line with the discussion of technologically mediated communication, this concept can be defined as follows (see also Swann and Husted, 2017):

> *Many-to-many communication* refers to the communication that takes place in networks where everyone participating is able to send and receive information to and from everyone else in the network. The technological mediation of many-to-many communication would include wikis, blogs, social media platforms, online chatrooms and, potentially, micro-blogging sites.

Social media, in so far as it creates an environment in which decentralised and dispersed communication networks can function, is one of the key architectures that allow for many-to-many communication; and to the extent that these networked organisation forms mirror the kind of organisation anarchism is concerned with, social media can be explored as providing potential sites for anarchist politics. Importantly, however, many-to-many communication can be seen to operate in a range of different ways and through a range of different media, and like the concept of networks itself, its operation and application is not restricted to recent advances in communication technology. Traditional marketplaces, sports stadiums, graffiti and community notice boards can all be seen as instances of many-to-many communication (Jensen and Helles, 2011: 520). The agorae and assemblies of Ancient Greece could similarly be understood as facilitating forms of many-to-many communication, and doing so in ways that, albeit imperfectly, embody some of the democratic processes common to anarchist and radical politics (Graeber, 2013: 190–4).

As enablers of many-to-many communication, social media platforms – which have been described as 'architectures of participation' (O'Reilly, 2005) – will be the focus of this book, when communication is discussed in subsequent chapters. Accounts of the 2011 uprisings and other recent political mobilisations that have embodied network dynamics have suggested that such social media technologies played an important role. Media theorist Geert Lovink characterises the social media platform as having three core functions: 'it is easy to use, it facilitates sociality, and it provides users with free publishing and production platforms that allow them to upload content in any form, be it pictures, video, or text' (Lovink, 2011: 5).

A central aspect, that we need to appreciate in understanding the roles of social media in the context of many-to-many communication and networked organisation, is its participatory nature, with the 'social' component of the term providing reference to a participatory and collaborative account of sociality; social media is participatory and collaborative in terms of both its communicative function, and its production. While I will not focus on it here, this notion of users of social media content as also its producers is important. As Michael Mandiberg puts it, 'from the audience's perspective, in order to experience the [social media platform] you *have to become a media producer*' (2012: 1, emphasis in original). Marisol Sandoval and Christian Fuchs also emphasise the importance of this productive aspect of social media engagement, linking it to the social through the idea of co-operation: 'individuals have certain cognitive features that they use to interact with others so that shared spaces of interaction are created. In some cases, these spaces are used not just for communication, but for the co-production of novel qualities of overall social systems and for community building' (Fuchs and Sandoval, 2014: 6).

It is against this backdrop of their potential roles in many-to-many communication, that social media platforms have been linked to radical left organisation. Authors such as those already mentioned – Castells, Mason, Juris – have written of the benefits that social media and many-to-many communication can provide for the kind of horizontal organising common in recent social movements. In contrast, several other authors – including Terranova (2000), Jarrett (2008), Morozov (2011) and Fuchs (2014) – have emphasised some of the negative aspects of social media platforms, that mitigate against this networked, non-hierarchical organisation. In Chapter 7 I will discuss some of these critiques of the use of social media in more detail. For now, it is enough to note how the corporate control of social media platforms and the harvesting of data for profit and manipulating user behaviour have been highlighted as key areas of concern. This has led to calls for social media platforms to either be nationalised and run by the state or brought under some other form of democratic control, such as ownership by users. Further, concrete responses to these critiques by activists have sought to embody ownership and control patterns along more democratic lines and there has been an increased focus on precisely how platforms might better support radical organising. One of the aims of this book is to outline how social media platforms can act as infrastructures to support effective anarchist organisation. As I will show throughout, turning to cybernetics, a science of organisation and communication, will be central to this.

Conclusion

In this chapter, I have outlined in broad terms the two core concerns of this book: organisation and communication. For the anarchist tradition in general, as well as for how I develop the idea of anarchist cybernetics here, organisation primarily concerns efforts to enshrine the autonomy of both individuals and groups within structures, in ways that allow for coherent political decision making. Indeed, one of anarchism's defining features historically has been its opposition to centralising tendencies, including their prominence in many of its fellow socialist and communist movements. While many, although not all, Marxists have favoured hierarchical and centralised political parties and focused on taking control of state power, for anarchists these forms of organisation and struggle continue to represent key sources of the kinds of domination they want to see eliminated. In acting prefiguratively, where the means of struggle need to reflect the ends they seek to achieve, anarchists have developed forms of organisation, such as federalism, that have embodied non-domination and anti-capitalism, as well as attempts to address intersecting oppressions such as patriarchy, white supremacy and colonialism. Communication practices, in relation to these anarchist approaches to organisation, can be seen as functional aspects of how participatory and democratic decision making is realised. Networked, many-to-many forms of communication are central, and social media platforms have played an important role, both in making anarchist organising possible in recent years and in highlighting how we might envision and create the kinds of platforms that better support this kind of decision making. In the chapters that follow, I focus on these two sides of anarchist cybernetics in turn, exploring organisation and (democratic) control in Chapters 4 and 5 and communication in Chapters 6 and 7. First, though, I want to elaborate on the connections between anarchism and cybernetics that shape how questions of control and communication might best be responded to.

3

Anarchism and Cybernetics: A Missed Opportunity Revisited

As the previous chapter highlighted, the idea of participatory and democratic self-organisation is at the centre of how radical left politics has developed in recent years, as witnessed both in how the Occupy camps and the related mobilisations of 2011 were structured, and in the role social media and other digital platforms have played in these and other forms of organising. And as we have seen, this type of approach already has an established position in anarchism's prefigurative account of politics and of self-organisation. It is through the concept of self-organisation that I want to draw a connection between anarchism, on the one hand, and the field of organisational cybernetics, on the other. In the introductory chapter, I briefly discussed the meaning of the term cybernetics (importantly, including a discussion of what it does not mean), and outlined some of the core features that make cybernetics sit particularly well alongside anarchism, even if that might initially appear to be an odd relationship. In this chapter, I will attempt to draw out these common features in more detail and ultimately present an initial picture of anarchist cybernetics, as a concept central to animating the discussions that follow in the book. This is a task that involves exploring aspects of the technical side of cybernetics, hopefully in ways that make its relevance for questions of social and political organisation obvious. At the heart of this conversation between anarchism and cybernetics is the idea of the Viable Systems Model as articulated by Stafford Beer, one of the key figures in the history of cybernetics I draw on in this book.

One possible history of cybernetics

In a book of this length, where the focus is on extrapolating the connections between cybernetics and anarchism and exploring what these might mean for radical forms of organisation, recounting the history of cybernetics in any great depth is not going to be possible. There are other books that do just that, and I will point the reader towards them at various points, particularly in this chapter. It is worth emphasising that there is not one agreed upon history of cybernetics; rather, cybernetics is best understood through multiple histories, each in their own way influenced by the contexts in which they were written, including the various influences of the social and political cleavages of the post-World War Two era. It is also worth noting that cybernetics is less a single coherent field and more a collection of different strands of academic and scientific development, that at some points bear little more than a rough family resemblance. What they share in common is a concern with how systems are regulated, but even this point of convergence is interpreted and actualised in different ways, in different places and at different times, by different groups of people. How cybernetics was initially approached as a science was strongly influenced or determined by the Cold War antagonism between the United States and the Soviet Union. In the latter, for instance, under Stalin's regime, cybernetics was rejected as Western pseudo-science, but then rehabilitated after his death and for a time seen as a prospective orthodoxy for running a centralised, planned economy using the advanced computing technology of the time. In the US, cybernetics was similarly influenced by political priorities and was shaped by strong links to the military and the CIA.

A parallel history of cybernetics identifies it with a countercultural radicalism that, in stark contrast, situates it outside and, at several key points, in opposition to both a US-dominated post-war political and economic hegemony and Soviet authoritarianism. It is through this history, exemplified for example in Andrew Pickering's book *The Cybernetic Brain* (2010), that the relationship with anarchist ideas of self-organisation comes to the fore. It is a history that, beginning with the work of Norbert Wiener during and immediately after World War Two, moves at speed through the post-war boom and innovations in management and organisation science, to the tragedy of Salvador Allende's socialist government in Chile, to a cottage in Wales without electricity or running water, through to explorations of the kinds of democratic structures that sit far more comfortably with anarchist ideals of organisation than either the Soviet or US mainstreams of cybernetic science do. To the extent that I want to draw on this history here – and I should stress that this is an extremely partial presentation, tailored towards underlining connections with how anarchists have viewed self-organisation – it is a story that can be told through the experiences of one man: Stafford Beer. It was Beer who picked up on the potential of cybernetics for understanding organisational effectiveness and he linked this directly to structures and functions of decision making. It is such links that allow us to constructively combine a technical appreciation of self-organisation with self-organisation understood in terms of participatory and democratic organisation.

Stafford Beer and the radicalisation of cybernetics

Beer was born in England in 1926 and after working with operations management in the British army in India founded the Operational Research Group at a Sheffield-based subsidiary of United Steel before running their Cybernetics Group. It was during this time, from the mid-1950s onwards, that Beer developed what would eventually become his Organisational Cybernetics, publishing three books on management and cybernetics. Alongside self-organisation, two of the central concepts in Beer's work are 'complexity' and 'control'.

In his first book, *Cybernetics and Management* (1967), Beer identified a number of different types of systems. These ranged from simple and deterministic systems (the dynamics of which we can fairly easily understand and that are largely predictable, such as how billiard balls move around a table) to exceedingly complex and probabilistic systems (that are difficult to understand and potentially impossible to predict, such as the brain, the economy, or forms of social organisation). Beer described this latter type of system as 'so complex and so probabilistic that it does not seem reasonable to imagine that it will ever be fully described' (1967: 17). The kinds of system he was interested in, and that are relevant to discussions of anarchist organisation, are these highly complex systems that are impossible or near-impossible to predict. Crucially, for Beer and with respect to cybernetics more generally, this complexity and this inability to accurately describe and predict the behaviour of such a system does not mean that controlling or managing it is impossible. In such contexts, control is defined as both attempting to reduce the complexity of the system and responding to it. Because it is impossible to fully map or describe an exceedingly complex system, responding to its complexity cannot involve a control function that operates with an overview of everything that is happening in the system. Instead, for cybernetics, control involves the various parts of the system working semi-autonomously to respond to their own area of complexity. Rather than a single controller trying to understand and respond to the complexity of the entire system, the different parts of the system each operate in relation to the smaller amount of complexity in their own area and are thus able to respond to complexity effectively and in doing so, together allow the wider system to achieve its goals.

Towards the end of the 1960s, Beer expanded this account of complexity and control to explore in more detail how organisations could function effectively by embracing the autonomy of their parts. Beer was now working as a management consultant, and the draft of his book *The Brain of the Firm* came to the attention of economists working for Salvador Allende's socialist government in Chile. Allende was elected as president of Chile in 1970 and a central aspect of his socialist programme involved reforming the Chilean economy to ensure that it worked more efficiently to meet the needs of the population. For Beer, who was invited to advise Allende's government in 1971, this meant shifting the focus of his cybernetics from a single organisation to an entire economy, or at least to the productive aspect of that economy. The intricacies of this project, dubbed Project Cybersyn, are covered in Eden Medina's *Cybernetic Revolutionaries* (2011). For the purpose of this fleeting overview of Beer's work, the important point to grasp is that Project Cybersyn involved designing and implementing a networked communications system that allowed the units of production (factories) to respond to information about the overall state of the system (the economy). Given the widespread impact of the internet in the decades since, it is easy to underestimate the importance of developing such a communications network. At the time, however, this represented one of the first examples of anything like this kind of project on this scale; indeed, it is commonly identified as one of the predecessors of the internet. With the limited technology available, Allende's government was able to utilise this communication network to, for example, resist a strike by lorry owners and other private business interests. This was not done through a centralised command operation but by Chilean workers maintaining supply chains, made possible by the networked form of communication Project Cybersyn was trying to build. A CIA-backed coup in 1973 resulted in the death of Allende and the destruction of his government's programme, including Project Cybersyn. Chile was plunged into a brutal dictatorship that promptly instituted widespread neoliberal economic programmes.

The Cybersyn experience had a profound effect on Beer. He entered that period of his life as a consultant accustomed to first-class travel and Rolls Royce cars. Shortly after the fall of Allende and the subsequent end of Project Cybersyn he turned his back on this extravagant lifestyle and moved to a cottage in the Welsh countryside that lacked running water or electricity. His work on cybernetics, however, did not stop there. He continued to publish on the topic and maintained contact with others working on cybernetics, living with his wife and fellow cybernetician Allenna Leonard, partly in Wales and partly in Toronto, from the 1980s until his death in 2002. While Beer was certainly no radical, his work post-Chile did take a turn away from narrower applications of cybernetics towards an increasingly broad focus on how cybernetic principles might help to inform the effective governance of society as a whole. In *Designing Freedom*, a book published in 1974, based on a series of radio lectures, Beer rails against a world system designed to produce consumption and misery and, in terms that would not be unfitting in the contemporary context of climate crisis, destined for catastrophic collapse:

> We spend our days boxed in our houses, swarming in and out of office blocks like tribes of ants, crammed into trains, canned into aeroplanes, locked solid in traffic jams on the freeway. Our unbiblical concern for what we shall eat, what we shall drink, and what we shall put on is amplified and made obsessional by the pressure to consume – way, way beyond the natural need. All this is demanded by the way we have arranged our economy. And the institutions we have built to operate that economy, to safeguard ourselves, protect our homes, care for and educate our families, have all grown into large and powerful pieces of social machinery which suddenly seem not so much protective as actually threatening. (Beer, 1974: 1)

Central to Beer's work is the Viable System Model, a concept introduced in *The Brain of the Firm* ([1981] 1994) and that framed how his organisational cybernetics approached questions of complexity and control, through rooting an organisation's responses to these in autonomy and self-organisation. I want to return to the cybernetic idea of self-organisation and how it relates to anarchism later in this chapter, but before doing so I need to explain more about what the Viable System Model is and how it helps us understand ways in which an organisation can effectively respond to complexity.

The Viable System Model

The trilogy of books that sit at the heart of Beer's literary output – *The Brain of the Firm* (first edition published in 1972, updated in 1981), *The Heart of the Enterprise* ([1979] 1994) and *Diagnosing the System for Organizations* (1985) – present what Beer called the Viable System Model (henceforth, VSM) as a method for understanding how control can operate in organisations to respond to complexity. Crucially, the organisation or system is divided into five sub-systems, each performing a different functional role that together allow the organisation as a whole to respond to complexity, both in the environment that surrounds it and in the organisation itself. Figure 1 illustrates how the different parts link up with one another and how they interact with the external environment.

System One – Primary activities

These represent the parts of the organisation that are in operation, working directly on specific tasks within the external environment. There can be any number of these in an organisation and they have the autonomy to respond to changes in their specific environmental niches as they see fit.

System Two – Coordination

The framework that covers the System One units in communication with one another and allows them to coordinate their activities. This provides a minimum level of coherence to the System One operations and helps avoid clashes and conflict but does not, on its own, afford them any organisational direction in terms of overarching goals.

System Three – Self-regulation

This is the first part of the system that is concerned with these overarching goals and regulates the operations of the System One units in accordance with the organisation as a whole. As Beer put it, Systems One and Two have to do with 'recognizing that there are other autonomous divisions other than my own', while Systems Three, Four and Five entail 'recognizing that my own autonomous division is part of a corporation' ([1981] 1994: 165). System Three performs an auditing function (often referred to as System Three*) on System

Figure 1: Viable System Model

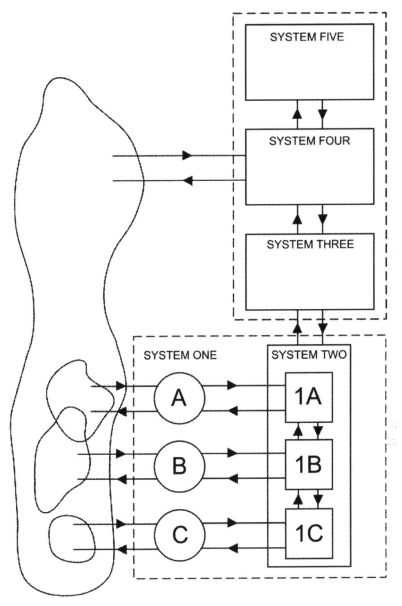

Notes: The diagram shows three System One units (A, B, C) and their interaction with both their local environmental niches and one another (1A, 1B, 1C), their coordination under System Two and the strategic alignment of the whole organisation or system at Systems Three, Four (in relation to the whole environment) and Five. The arrows represent communication and action between the different parts. The dotted lines indicate the two sections of the model.

Source: Based on Beer's depiction ([1981] 1994: 128); see also Beer and Leonard, 2019.

One and Two units, providing a mechanism for regulation in line with the overall organisation.

System Four – Awareness

The concern here is for the immediate strategy of the organisation, taking into account information about the activities of other parts of the system (from System Three), from the external environment and from System Five.

System Five – Identity

Drawing a parallel with human physiology, Beer describes this as 'the thinking part of the whole organisation' ([1981] 1994: 201) which is focused on long-term strategic planning, taking information from System Four and developing the overall goals and ethos of the organisation. Only in extreme circumstances does it take direct action on other parts of the organisation.

The VSM, as Beer describes, has many characteristics that can be applied to a blueprint for organisation, something that is designed by experts like Beer and then applied in order to structure an organisation according to the sub-systems just described. Given that the aim of this book is to outline the possibility of an anarchist cybernetics, the idea of the VSM as a plan or blueprint should surely run up against the common rejection in the anarchist tradition of blueprints and grand ideas for how society should be structured. For anarchism, having a blueprint for a future society, or even for anarchist organisations, is counter to the commitment to people collectively shaping the world they live in. If a blueprint exists, worked out in advance and then applied by those experts who understand it best, then that limits the scope of people to have any real control over how they operate together. For Beer, however, the VSM is not in fact intended as a blueprint in this sense. Rather, he describes it as a 'diagnostic tool' ([1981] 1994: 155), a conception that is echoed in cybernetician Roger Harnden's framing of it as a 'hermeneutic enabler' (1989). Rather than being a strict plan as to how a system or organisation must be designed, the VSM works as a map of sorts, one that is aimed at helping people navigate the organisations they are working with(in). It highlights the requirements for effective organisation in terms of functions and lines of communication but does not prescribe any specific structure. The different sub-systems correspond to certain functions and not, as we will see shortly, different, discrete parts of an organisation.

Requisite variety, control and self-organisation

One of the defining features of cybernetics, then, is that it shows ways in which systems and organisations can respond to complexity through control, and in doing so provides a unique understanding of control. A key way this is framed in cybernetics is through the concept of 'requisite variety'. This is often called the Law of Requisite Variety or, after its founder Ross Ashby, Ashby's Law; this states that for any system to remain stable and to operate effectively in its environment, the system itself must display the same level of variety and flexibility as that of the environment that it operates in (Ashby, 1956; [1958] 2003). The environments that systems and organisations exist in will inevitably change over time. This is a fundamental assumption of cybernetics. Such changes, in this context, are referred to as complexity or variety. In digital contexts, where environments will shift between discrete states, there will be a specific and potentially calculatable number of possible states. Thus, the variety of a system can be given a specific figure, reflecting the number of different possible states the environment can be in. The concept of requisite variety provides an understanding as to why a system or organisation will need to have the same number of possible states so that it can change in response to changes in the environment. For cybernetics, the ability of systems or organisations to do this, to have the same variety as the environments they exist in and so to have the potential for changing as the environment changes and thus not be overwhelmed by complexity, is vital if those systems and organisations are to be able to regulate themselves effectively.

A commonly used example that helps explain this is the thermostat. A room with a heater and a thermostat will be comprised of a system (constituted of these three parts) and an environment (the air in the room, with a changing temperature). The thermostat both measures the variety in the environment (the air temperature) and regulates the behaviour of the system (through its ability to turn the heater on or off). As the environment changes (gets hotter or colder) the thermostat will respond by changing the behaviour of the heater (either on to heat the room or off to cool it). The variety in the environment will be determined by factors such as the time of year and the weather, but the possible states of the environment will be limited to a set range. In any particular region of the world the temperature will range between given extremes; obviously extremes that are now in flux due to climate change, but within a set range nonetheless. The thermostat, to be able to appropriately respond to changes in temperature and thus maintain the room at a desirable level, needs to have the capacity to both measure and act in response to any possible change. If the temperature rises beyond or sinks below the predicted extremes, for example during an unusually cold period – when the variety in the system may be unable to match the variety in the environment and the system will be overwhelmed – the heater will be unable to heat the room sufficiently because the environment is colder than the lowest temperature provided for in its range of responses.

This process, where complexity or change in the environment is responded to effectively because the system or organisation has the requisite variety to match the variety in the environment, is what is understood as control in cybernetics. As Beer puts it, control means 'capable of adapting smoothly to change' (1974: 88). Any viable system will be able to both attenuate variety in its environment (reduce variety so that the system can comprehend and respond effectively to it) and amplify its own variety (increase its capacity to match the variety in the environment). Importantly, with respect to attenuating and amplifying variety through this kind of control process in social systems – organisations involving people working together – it is a far less technical affair than the thermostat example might suggest. As cyberneticians Angela Espinosa, Roger Harnden and Jon Walker put it, 'the internal dynamics of the organisation and the external niche [the environment] change in a never-ending dance' (2008: 640). While emphasising the quantitative nature of requisite variety, Ashby in fact defined control in similar terms, likening it to fencers responding to each other's moves and attacks ([1958] 2003: 356). Allena Leonard provides a particularly useful definition of control in cybernetics with specific relation to organisation:

> A cybernetic understanding is not the control that is backed up by coercion [...] It is the control of a skier going down a hill, of balancing this way and that. Or it is the control of a helmsman steering a ship. The one thing that people do not realize about [cybernetics] is that the control is in each function, not top-down [...] That makes cybernetics more of a science of balancing than a science of control. (Leonard, 2013: 16–17)

The example of the thermostat is also not an ideal one to relate to the cybernetics of social organisation because the control function in that example can be identified as a single point in the system. The thermostat itself is the aspect with agency that directs how the system responds to change. Like Leonard, Beer is very clear that control does not function in a top-down manner and is not an activity that is the preserve of a 'controller' part of the organisation. He writes, for example, that '[t]he controller is not something stuck on to a system by a higher authority which then accords it managerial prerogatives. [...] the control function is spread throughout the architecture of the system' ([1981] 1984: 35). It is in this sense, then, that self-organisation is defined as a concept in cybernetics. While, as with control, it has a technical definition in cybernetics, self-organisation can also be understood in very simple terms as the ability of systems and organisations to regulate or control themselves without the need of a centralised or external controller. Stewart Umpleby (1987) outlines the distinction involved here:

> A teacher can organize a class into groups by assigning each child to a specific group and picking the group leaders. She could also tell the children to organize themselves into groups of five and then let them get on with it in a self-organizing fashion. (Umpleby, 1987)

Pertaining to social organisation, therefore, cybernetics highlights how people can organise themselves in ways that both eschew centralised control and, crucially, allows those people and the organisation as a whole to operate effectively in response to the complexity and variety of the environments they operate within.

In his book *Beyond Dispute. The Invention of Team Syntegrity*, published in 1994, Beer makes a distinction between government and governance. Government, he says, is often considered as 'intrinsically totalitarian, autocratic and reprehensible'. He goes on, '[f]ortunately for a cybernetician, governance is a quality of self-organizing systems, and is not an imposition from outside' (Beer, 1994: 165). As I will show later, with further discussion of this throughout the book, this is a distinction that is helpful in explaining how anarchists might view self-organisation and democracy. Government entails control as domination; governance, on the other hand, *can* operate in the form of control as self-organisation. Towards the end of his career, Beer conceived of a process, which he called 'syntegration' that was aimed at allowing people to effectively self-organise and make decisions. This draws on Buckminster Fuller's mathematical modelling of the tensile integrity of geodesic spheres to allow for a group of 30 people, termed an 'infoset' to arrive at a common agreement on an issue. Through a detailed process of back and forth communication, Beer writes,

> what everyone is saying to everyone else, within the team, within the critical apparatus, and having regard to polar opposites, [...] is constantly rebounding around the group. [...] *The Conclusion* is meant to be a convergence on twelve [final statements], with the whole Infoset in agreement. (Beer, 1994: 33, emphasis in original)

Beer was involved in several experiments focused on this syntegration process, covering academia, business and community development. Syntegration follows a series of steps that are aimed at moving the group from their initially disparate opinions on a topic to a shared and informed position (Beer, 1994: 19–34). As originally formulated, the process, or 'protocol' as Beer calls it, should take place over several days and in person, although he suggests that groups mediated by communications technologies and so potentially separated by great distances may be possible. Participants begin by writing down statements of importance. These can concern anything that the participant wants but should be, to some extent, provocative. Facilitators consider the statements and eliminate any duplicates, before providing a list of statements to the participants. Five 'Problem Jostle' sessions take place, during which 12 composite statements of importance are developed, to subsequently provide the agenda for the protocol as a whole. Each of these topics is then subjected to a series of discussions involving their promoters and their critics. Through these engagements, in which participants take part in multiple discussions around the 12 statements, patterns of interaction and creative thinking are established. Facilitators help these discussions converge on outcome statements that represent a group's shared agreements on the key topics that they have decided to discuss (see Leonard, 1996 for an additional overview). Syntegration thus represents a possible procedural approach to making self-organisation in groups of people a reality.

Second-order cybernetics

As already mentioned, technical discussions of self-organised systems view the concept differently from how we might deploy it in everyday life and with reference to social organisation. Ashby goes so far as to argue that self-organisation is in fact something that cannot be said to exist (1962; see also von Foerster, [1960] 2003). He suggests that when we speak of systems as self-organised, what we are really saying is that from a particular perspective it appears to be self-organised. As such, self-organisation is not a property of systems but of our observations of them. A thermostat does not, of course, have the kind of agency that we might commonly attribute to something that we view as self-organised. It is self-regulating, but it is set up by agencies external to it (the people who fitted the thermostat and heater in the room) and the variables in its behaviour are set in advance. It has not decided to organise itself in a certain way, to achieve the goal of maintaining a particular temperature in the room. It is only self-organised in the sense that, once set in motion, it regulates itself and does not require an external controller to measure the temperature and decide to turn the heater on and off as required. But in the context of social systems, such as organisations where people come together to work on something collectively, the agency is located within the system and the process of self-organisation is genuinely one of people organising their affairs together, without outside control. Here, self-organisation is something that actually exists in the system, not just an aspect of how it can be observed in a specific, technical way.

Nonetheless, this point about observation is an important one for cyberneticians and for understanding cybernetics. Early in its history, a distinction was made between first-order and second-order cybernetics. While first-order cybernetics saw systems as existing objectively, independent of observation, second-order cybernetics held that systems exist only as they are observed, and so the observer is necessarily a key part of any description of the system. This distinction was originally drawn in the work of scholars including Margaret Mead and Heinz von Foerster, who attended the Macey Conferences that helped establish cybernetics as a scientific discipline (Mead, 1968; von Foerster, [1991] 2003). It is based on a 'radical constructivist' philosophy of knowledge (von Glaserfeld, 1991) whereby 'our observations are not direct observations of a "reality", rather they are constructions based on particular sets of assumptions' (Scott, 2004: 1374). This development in cybernetics has been influential both in a number of attempts aimed at expanding this field of study and as to how it and systems theory more generally have been applied to social and political problems. The work of Humberto Maturana and Francisco Varela (1980), Niklas Luhmann (1995) and Katherine Hayles (1999) are of particular interest in this regard. While I do not have sufficient space to explore these different avenues taken by cybernetics and systems theory in any detail here, I do want to point out why this second-order cybernetics approach to understanding systems is important for the argument of this book.

Following Pickering (2010), I draw on Beer's cybernetics here as an example of second-order cybernetics (in contrast to Timon Beyes, 2005, who argues that Beer's is a first-order cybernetics). What this insight of second-order cybernetics means for this discussion of organisation is that the observations made of systems and organisations, rather than being representations of objective reality, can be understood as constructions that are able to aid people in analysing and structuring the systems they operate as part of. As I have already mentioned in this chapter, Beer's VSM is intended in just this way: not as an accurate image of organisation, a blueprint that can be copied, but as a tool used to improve organisational effectiveness. For Pickering, key to this is the idea of performance, defined as actions that people take in the world that involve this kind of pragmatic construction of reality. Knowledge, Pickering argues, is considered a '*part of* performance rather than as an external control of it' (2010: 25, emphasis in original). In so far as cybernetics is a science that aims to produce knowledge, it is not involved in unpacking and describing reality but rather with people, as observers and participants, constructing knowledge as a way of facilitating the performances, or practices, they are involved in. The ontology of second-order cybernetics – in other words, the way cybernetics understands what reality is – is described by Pickering as an 'ontology of becoming', where truth and knowledge are constructed by people doing things together. As they act, or perform as Pickering puts it, they develop knowledge relative to and through that acting or performance.

Returning to the thermostat example, we can see how this approach to knowledge and reality plays a role in self-organised systems. When we set a thermostat to a certain temperature, we normally set it at one of a number of possible, discrete values: 22.5°C or 23°C, for example. The thermostat will also read the temperature in the room in a similar way, as being at a discrete level. If we think about how air temperature or room temperature actually exists, however, we need to understand it in terms of a continuous and fluctuating range. When the thermostat says that the current temperature is 19°C, this is an approximation of what the thermostat is sensing and might mean that the temperature is closer to 19°C than any other possible value the thermostat can display. If we had a more expensive thermostat, it might read 18.8°C. In both cases, however, what the thermostat is doing is reducing the variety in the environment from that of a continuous scale to a range of possible discrete values. It does so in order to effectively function and heat or cool the room. A traditional thermometer, with liquid mercury that expands or contracts could be said to provide a more accurate representation of temperature, because it functions in terms of a continuous range, but for it to be useful we still need to be able to look at it and say 'it's roughly 19°C'. The knowledge that is produced in these examples is not a direct representation of an objective reality but a construction that is useful to the people or to the system involved. The variety is constructed in a way that allows the system to function effectively in terms of its purpose.

Beer describes a similar process called 'variety attenuation', which functions to turn a level of change or complexity on a continuous range into a discrete number of possible states. This can also be understood in terms of the difference between analogue and digital. An analogue watch, as far as our use of it is concerned, continuously turns so that we can roughly judge where the minute hand is to tell the time. A digital watch, on the other hand, gives discrete readings, where we can say at any given moment what the hour, minute and second is. This helps us to construct our knowledge of the time in a way that we might find more practically useful than that constructed by an analogue representation. The possible states of the environment, if we consider time an external environment, are attenuated to a set number of discrete possibilities. Depending on our purpose – in Pickering's terms, the performance we are engaged in – we might require higher or lower levels of attenuation. In timing laps in a race, we might need a level of attenuation that is as precise as the millisecond or smaller, where there may be 60,000 possible states in every minute. In running a school timetable, on the other hand, a level of attenuation with minutes, with only 1,440 possible states in every 24 hours, might suffice. The point here is that the knowledge we use in any given situation, and for cybernetics in any system or organisation, is, through processes like attenuation, constructed to meet the needs of that situation, system or organisation. Reality is not something that is objective but something we co-construct with other people when we act or perform together.

Anarchism and cybernetics

While Beer himself was certainly no anarchist, the theoretical relationship between organisational cybernetics and the self-organisation that is central to anarchism has long been acknowledged. In 1963, the journal *Anarchy*, edited by the prominent post-war British anarchist Colin Ward, included two contributions on cybernetics. The first of these, from neurophysiologist Grey Walter, dealt primarily with physiology and robotics, only very briefly turning to the question of social or political organisation. Walter was responsible for some of the earliest robots to display elements of self-organisation. In the late 1940s he developed the tortoise, a device that was able to follow a light source without any external control by using photoreceptors (Pickering, 2010). Although the tortoise's behaviour was, as Beer might have put it, simple and deterministic, it nonetheless successfully demonstrated how an artificial system could achieve a goal in a complex environment without a person being on hand to guide it. Grey Walter's son, Nicholas, was, along with Ward, a figure central within anarchism in the UK at the time, and Grey's father, Karl, attended the 1907 Anarchist Congress in Amsterdam. While there is little to suggest that Grey Walter shared as strong a commitment to anarchism as either his father or son, he was attentive to the relationship between the cybernetics of self-organisation and anarchist politics. In his article in *Anarchy*, he wrote of physiology that 'we find no boss in the brain, no oligarchic ganglion or glandular Big Brother' (Walter, 1963: 89). He added:

> Within our heads, our lives depend on equality of opportunity, on specialisation with versatility, on free communication and just restraint, a freedom without interference. Here too local minorities can and do control their own means of production and expression in free and equal intercourse with their neighbours. If we must identify biological and political systems our own brains would seem to illustrate the capacity and limitations of an anarcho-syndicalist community. (Walter, 1963: 89)

This passage mirrors a similar statement from Beer on how control can be understood in cybernetics through the self-regulating and self-organising qualities of viable systems:

> There is no ultimate ganglion in the brain that tells the nervous system what to do. There is no thermostat anywhere in the body with a marker set at the temperature 98.4F. And the *Book of Proverbs* reminds that 'the locusts have no kind, and yet they go about in bands'. In short, democratic systems regulate and organise themselves without benefit of dictate or ukase. They do not have hierarchies of command. (Beer, [1975] 2009: 25)

Beer goes so far as to describe these systems as anarchic, 'which is to say', he comments, 'without a ruler, and that is the literal meaning of anarchy'; and the processes of control that cybernetics uncovers are characterised by Beer as 'Laws of Anarchy' ([1975] 2009). For both Beer and Walter, then, while never developed fully in their work, there were clear lines of connection drawn between their cybernetic accounts of self-organisation and ideas of democratic and non-hierarchical decision making.

In response to Walter's article in *Anarchy*, a letter appeared in a subsequent issue from John D. McEwan and was quickly followed quickly by a full article later in the year. Both the letter and the article expanded on these connections, drawing on insights from Beer's work and explicitly linking these to how anarchist organisation functions. To my knowledge McEwan did not publish anything on anarchism, or indeed on any other topic, either before or after this 1963 article in *Anarchy* (which was republished in 1987 in a collection of articles from the journal) and I have failed to find any information about his life or work other than that he graduated from St Andrews University and worked in Manchester in the then-emerging field of robotics. His limited contribution to the anarchist canon could not be in greater contrast to its importance in how I want to develop the idea of Anarchist Cybernetics here. His article explores the relationship between cybernetics and anarchist organisation and lays the foundations for the anarchist approach to effective democratic organisation that I elaborate on in this book. McEwan begins by highlighting the fundamental overlap between anarchism and cybernetics already identified by Walter:

> The basic premise of the governmentalist – namely, that any society must incorporate some mechanisms for overall control – is certainly true, if we use 'control' in the sense of 'maintain a large number of critical variables within limits of tolerance'. [...] The error of the governmentalist is to think that 'incorporate some mechanism for control' is always equivalent to 'include a fixed isolatable control unit to which the rest, i.e. the majority, of the system is subservient'. This may be an adequate interpretation in the case of a model railway system, but not for a human society. The alternative model is complex, and changing in it search for stability in the face of unpredictable disturbances. (McEwan, [1963] 1987: 57)

McEwan compares this cybernetic account of control and self-organisation to a comment from Peter Kropotkin's (1898) work 'Anarchism: Its Philosophy and Ideal' on the concept of anarchist society, 'which looks for harmony in an ever-changing and fugitive equilibrium between a multitude of varied forces' (quoted in McEwan, [1963] 1987: 52). Indeed, Kropotkin argued elsewhere for anarchism in terms that would not be out of place in a discussion of control and requisite variety. He wrote, for instance, that 'in all production there arise daily thousands of difficulties which no government can solve or foresee' and that 'production and exchange represented an undertaking so complicated that the plans of the state socialists, which inevitably to a party dictatorship, would prove to be absolutely ineffective as soon as they were applied to life' (Kropotkin, 1927: 76–7). Here, Kropotkin restates the anarchists' opposition to revolutionary change through the seizing of centralised state power on the grounds that such an authority would be unable to respond to the complexity of a large-scale economy. This crucial connection between anarchism and cybernetics with respect to self-organisation and achieving harmony in the face of complexity can be found throughout the anarchist tradition, with Ward, for example, identifying this line of thinking as early as the work of Pierre-Joseph Proudhon. Ward cites cybernetics in his (1966) work, presumably following his introduction to it at the hands of Walter and McEwan, stating that '[h]armony results not from unity but from complexity [...] Anarchy is a function not of society's simplicity and lack of social organisation, but of its complexity and multiplicity of social organisations' (1973: 50). Again, anarchist self-organisation is defended on terms that resonate strongly with cybernetic notions of requisite variety and control.

Functional hierarchy

What is most important in McEwan's article on anarchism and cybernetics, however, is not how he characterises the connections between the traditions with respect to the concepts of self-organisation and control, but his proposals as to the implications for organisational structure. Key to this discussion is the specific form of hierarchy at work in the VSM and in cybernetics more generally and the vital distinction that needs to be drawn between functional and anatomical hierarchy. While the relationship between anarchism and cybernetics never progressed beyond that which was discussed in McEwan's article and a handful of subsequent comments on the topic by Ward and others (see, for example, Dolgoff, 1989; Kinna, 2005; Goodman, 2010; Barrington-Bush, 2013; Duda, 2013; De Geus, 2014), this distinction with respect to hierarchy sits at the heart of how I want to develop anarchist cybernetics. Returning to the VSM, as described earlier in this chapter, it is clear from the diagram provided that this, at least on paper, is a hierarchical model of organisation. The sub-systems are nested one on top of the other and numbered progressively from System One to System Five. For Beer, while autonomy was central to self-organisation, this autonomy was qualified. He wrote that while 'some part of any viable system does what it likes', to the extent that it is part of a viable system and not completely independent 'it does what it is told' (1974: 71). If anarchists can be considered to have a 'fanatical love of liberty' (Bakunin, 1871), then Beer's 'effective freedom' (1973) is a far less encompassing embrace of autonomy. I will explore this idea of effective freedom further in Chapter 5, but for now I want to focus on what this might mean for the hierarchical nature of the VSM and for the apparent clash between this hierarchy and the autonomy and democracy of anarchist politics. I propose that the answer is to be found in the contrast between functional and anatomical hierarchy.

McEwan wrote in his *Anarchy* article that in cybernetics, 'the usage [of the term "hierarchy"] is a technical one and does not coincide with the use of the term in anarchist criticism of political organisation' ([1963] 1987: 44). According to McEwan, the concept of anatomical hierarchy refers to what we normally understand by the term 'hierarchy': different levels in an organisation with a chain of command running between then and with lower levels subordinate to higher ones. This is hierarchy within the structure or anatomy of an organisation, hence McEwan calling it anatomical. Functional hierarchy, on the other hand, concerns a situation where 'there are two or more levels of information structure operating in the system' (McEwan, [1963] 1987: 44). This describes a distinction between two (or more) parts of a system or organisation, with the information and decision making at the higher part(s) necessarily concerning the lower part(s). As McEwan puts it, this is a hierarchy whereby 'some parts may deal directly with the environment, while other parts relate to the activity of these first parts'. In the discussion of the VSM earlier in this chapter, I noted that System Three, for example, is tasked with coordinating lower parts of the model, and similarly with respect to Systems Four and Five. This might still sound like a traditional hierarchy, what McEwan would describe an anatomical hierarchy. What is interesting in the VSM in this regard, however, is how these sub-systems can be maintained as *functions* in an organisation or system, without necessarily being constituted as anatomical or structural components of that organisation or system. To see why this is the case, we need to turn to another of the early cyberneticians.

The idea of functional hierarchy, and thus how McEwan uses this concept to relate Beer's cybernetics to anarchist organisation, has its origins in the work of Gordon Pask. Pask was, like Beer, an eccentric and incredibly insightful figure in the field of cybernetics, and later in this book I will return to his work on communication and the design of systems. For now, however, I want to focus on what he had to say about hierarchy. Unlike Beer's, Pask's work did not deal with management as such, but he did write about functional hierarchy, utilising the context of the firm to illustrate what he meant by the term:

> Imagine a busy executive (who acts as an overall controller in the hierarchy) disturbed by m callers. Each hour, to achieve stability and get on with his work, he engages a receptionists (who acts as a sub controller) [...] The receptionist [...] is able to perform the selective operation of prevaricating with callers so that, for example, the one who is welcome each hour is accepted [...] In a very real sense, which gives substance to the idea of a 'level', the interaction of sub controllers takes place in an object language (talking about receptionists). There can of course be any number of levels. (Pask, [1961] 1968: 61)

The point Pask is making here is that the hierarchy in the organisation, for example between the executive and the receptionist, is a hierarchy of levels of language as much as it is a structural hierarchy. At the highest level, the language is a metalanguage that is used to talk about lower level languages. For Pask, this involves a logical hierarchy of orders of language and is distinct from any structural or anatomical hierarchy that may be present. This hierarchy of functions is separable from the hierarchy of structure, as Pask goes on to argue:

> Each member must have the possibility, however small, of inverting the structure without leaving his [sic] niche to do so. I do not mean 'the office boy can rise to be manager'. I mean, 'in some unspecified conditions the office boy can take the managerial decisions'. (Pask, [1961] 1968: 111)

For anarchist cybernetics, the importance of this cannot be overstated. Beer's VSM, rather than identifying structural parts of an organisation, instead highlights the various functions that an organisation needs to fulfil in order to be viable – that is, to be effective in achieving its goals and maintaining equilibrium in its environment. While there are functions that are ordered hierarchically on top of one another, this does not mean that these functions must be assigned to hierarchically ordered parts of the organisation. As Pask says, there are managerial decisions that have to be made, but anyone, including those in structurally or anatomically lower parts of the organisation, can make those decisions. Beer was in fact disdainful of referring to higher and lower functions as 'senior management' and 'junior management' respectively, arguing that the hierarchy in the VSM is not 'equivalent to the political supposition that there must be policy bosses' and that the hierarchical relationship 'is a *logical* relationship, whatever social form it is given' ([1979] 1994: 130, emphasis in original). The functional hierarchy of decisions that are higher than, or come logically before, other decisions does not need to be replicated in an organisational structure that is itself hierarchical. This important distinction, between functional hierarchy and anatomical or structural hierarchy, is what opens up possibilities with respect to relationships between anarchism and the VSM and cybernetics more generally.

An anarchist VSM?

As I suggested in Chapter 1, Occupy Wall Street was in many ways archetypal of anarchist organisation, both in terms of the immediate goals it wanted to achieve and in how it developed over time, including with respect to the limitations and problems it encountered. There has been a wealth of debate on this topic, both during the time period of the camp's existence and in the years since. Rather than repeating and examining some of the arguments for and against the thesis that Occupy was anarchist, proceeding from an assumption that it was at least anarchistic in nature I want to take the terminology and basic structure of Occupy Wall Street as a basic framework for helping to articulate how an anarchist version of Beer's Viable System Model might work. So the aim, as I close this chapter, is not to present Occupy Wall Street as a real life model of an anarchist VSM, but instead to use it to provide some rough guidelines for the general structure of anarchist organisation, a structure that, I argue, is best understood through an appreciation of the VSM. This discussion is informed by accounts of Occupy from academics (many of them also participants in Occupy) such as David Graeber (2013), Marianne Maeckelbergh (2012; 2014) and Mark Bray (2013), as well as by activists (for example, Khatib et al., 2012). It is also based on my own close reading of the general assembly minutes from Occupy Wall Street that help chart some of how the camp changed over time (Kinna et al., 2019).

If we look back to the VSM as I presented it earlier in the chapter, the description there started with System One, the units tasked with the most fundamental activities of the organisation. In Occupy, these day-to-day activities that related to the basic running of the camp as well as the planning of protests and demonstrations were carried out by separate working groups. In Occupy Wall Street, for example, working groups were set up to cover tasks such as running the kitchen, dealing with the press, studying topics such as the economy and energy, producing propaganda and various forms of media, organising events and protests and dealing with legal issues. The working groups were where individual activists could volunteer to help out with different jobs in the camp and people could be members of more than one working group. As well as working groups, there were caucuses where participants from marginalised groups could meet and organise together. If we understand these working groups and caucuses as the basic System One units of the organisation, the units that have specific roles but in and of themselves are not yet coordinated as a whole system, then the first level of this coordination can be identified as both the simple, informal communication between groups (for example, in chats between activists over lunch) and communication in more formal settings (such as in meetings). From this understanding, it is already apparent that while there are two functional levels at work, with the System One activities logically below System Two coordination, these functions are not made manifest in a hierarchical structure. There is no System Two controller group that has formal authority over System One units. Instead, the functional hierarchy is achieved by way of a more or less horizontal organisational structure.

These two sub-systems (System One and System Two) are then brought into an overall organisation or system by the functions performed by the higher sub-systems in the model (Systems Three, Four and Five). When Occupy began, these logically or functionally higher tasks were performed by the general assembly. Auditing the activities of System One working groups and relating them to the goals of Occupy (System Three), drawing information from the surrounding environment and the camp as a whole (System Four) and utilising this information in the development and assessment of strategy (System Five) all took place in the general assembly meetings. These were meetings that took place almost every evening, sometimes twice in one day, which were open to anyone involved in the camp. So while there were different functions being performed throughout the various structures of the camp, crucially, the same individuals could be involved at all points of decision making in the structure. The same people engaging in the day-to-day activities of the working groups (System One) and coordinating these activities through informal and formal communication (System Two) could also potentially be involved in ensuring these activities were in line with the aims of the camp as a single organisation (System Three), feeding relevant knowledge into discussions concerning what was going on inside and outside the camp (System Four) and, finally, make decisions through consensus decision making about strategy (System Five).

Taking the Occupy Wall Street camp as a whole, then, we can see that the means of regulating overall behaviour and of controlling the system's activities was a complex process, one that involved different levels of function and different formal and informal structures. For anarchist cybernetics and the idea of an anarchist VSM, however, it is key to note that, first, these structures are not hierarchical in the way that the functions are and, second, that the same individuals can be involved in the full range of different structures that perform these various functions. In this sense, the model of the Occupy camp can be seen as an example of an anarchist Viable System Model in so far as it performs the functions identified in Beer's VSM, while manifesting them through non-hierarchical structures in which no one is subservient to anyone else or excluded from functionally higher levels of decision making. What is perhaps even more interesting with respect to Occupy Wall Street specifically is how changes that were made to the organisational structure towards the end of the camp's existence maintained both the functional hierarchy of the VSM and the horizontal democratic decision making of anarchism. As I mentioned previously, the general assembly was the site for System Three, four and five functions. Over time, the assembly became increasingly less able to perform the functions required of it, in part because anyone, whether they were actually involved in the camp or its working groups or not, could turn up and participate in the assembly, including tourists who had heard about the now-famous camp. By way of a solution, a spokes-council was proposed and set up to take over some of the functions of the general assembly, particularly with respect to coordination of the camp and the working groups. In practice, this involved delegates from working groups and caucuses making decisions to do with Systems Three and Four functions, with decisions as to strategy around politics and goals (System Five functions) remaining with the general assembly where anyone could participate (I will return to the spokes-council and its role in the following chapter). In terms of how cybernetics helps us understand self-organisation, this shift towards the spokes-council model can be understood as an attempt to cope with the excessive variety present in the general assembly. Such a large gathering, giving a platform to almost anyone present, produced more variety (in terms of proposals, discussion points, information about the camp and the environment, and so on) than the decision-making structure of the assembly was able to comfortably handle. The spokes-council can be seen, then, as a way of attenuating or limiting this variety so that the decision-making structure is able to cope and respond effectively. The general assembly, in turn, was reformulated to deal exclusively with System Five functions where high variety is perhaps less of a concern.

This embodiment of System Five in the general assembly, the forum open to all camp participants, neatly mirrors one of the most famous anecdotes Beer recounts about his time in Chile. In discussing his presentation of the VSM to Allende, Beer paints the following picture:

> [...] in relation to my first Chilean report, the remark came 'the government should be conceived as a viable system (System Five being the President of the Republic)'. I drew the square on the piece of paper labelled Five. [Allende] threw himself back in his chair: 'at last', he said, '*el pueblo*'. (Beer, [1981] 1994: 258)

'At last, the people.' From an anarchist standpoint, one may be sceptical as to the extent to which 'the people' was really in control, via a process of the election of the president and other representatives, but in so far as Allende, and from that moment on Beer himself, believed in the ability for a representative model of democracy to put the people in charge, this statement is vitally important. System Five, where overarching goals and political strategy is developed, is something that ought to be rooted in everyone involved in the system. For Allende the mechanism for realising this function was the election of representatives, with the population providing a mandate for a particular programme of government; for Occupy and indeed for anarchist organisation more broadly, it is direct participation that best puts those involved in control of the organisation.

Conclusion

It is undoubtedly true that Beer was no anarchist. In the second edition of *Brain of the Firm* ([1981] 1994), which included reflections on his involvement in Chile with Project Cybersyn, Beer is interested in the state as a viable system, and while he characterises the viable state as democratic, this is something antithetical to anarchism. In the one lecture where he discusses the anarchic nature of viable systems at any length – the 1979 lecture 'Laws of Anarchy' – he makes a distinction between democratic government, for example of the representative type he advised in Chile under Allende, and 'bomb-producing students' [1975] 2009: 33), which can be taken as a reference to the caricature of the anarchist in the popular imagination. For Beer, the democracy that existed in countries like Allende's Chile is 'without rulers' [1975] 2009: 25) and, in so far as anarchy involves regulation and organisation without top-down, centralised control, 'is where anarchy really lies' [1975] 2009: 33). In spite of Allende's proclamation that it was 'the people' and not him as president that was at the top of the system, describing representative democracy as anarchic and without rulers is something anarchists from Proudhon onwards would take issue with and is certainly at odds with how many involved in the 2011 uprisings saw ostensibly democratic systems in the US, Spain and elsewhere (as highlighted in the previous chapters).

Putting this (mis)application of the term 'anarchic' to liberal democracy to one side, it is worth noting that at his most political, Beer's writing often converges with some of anarchism's concerns for decentralisation and autonomy, concerns that will be explored throughout this book. Noting the need for a balance between centralisation and decentralisation (something that might at first strike us as decidedly un-anarchist but which in the following chapters I will show is consistent with anarchist politics), he writes that,

> it is clear that there should be a major devolution of power. I think it should be open to a community to organize its social services (education, health, welfare) exactly as it pleases, and to accept or reject the initiatives of local innovators. I think that goes for the local branches of national undertakings, public and private, also. I think that workers should in general be free to organize their own work, and that students (up to the age of death) should be free to organize their own studies. (Beer, 1974: 78–9)

Perhaps it is this, not necessarily conspicuous or immediately evident, spirit of Beer's work that makes his cybernetics so amenable to an anarchist reading.

By bringing cybernetics and anarchism together, it is possible to highlight the functions required of any successful and effective organisation – such as those articulated by Beer's Viable System Model – and show how these can be embodied in a non-hierarchical, participatory and democratic manner. Central to this is the distinction between the functional hierarchy that is discussed by cyberneticians like Pask and McEwan and that is the focus of Beer's model, on the one hand, and the structural or anatomical hierarchy which we normally think of when we use the term hierarchy. A focus on the importance of cybernetics for organisational questions helps to make clear that while both of these forms of hierarchy may well be present in many organisations, there is nothing to say that they both need to be for such organisations to be effective. Occupy Wall Street illustrates one way in which a functional hierarchy can be maintained in an organisation which aims to have a non-hierarchical (in terms of structural or anatomical hierarchy) structure. For anarchism, embracing cybernetics does not, therefore, have to involve a compromise with a position that rejects (structural or anatomical) hierarchy, because what is being embraced is a functional hierarchy that has nothing to do with structural hierarchy in organisational terms. An anarchist Viable Systems Model outlines how different functions can be performed in ways that involve some being logically or functionally higher in order than others, while maintaining a commitment to a non-hierarchical structure that allows for everyone to have a say at all levels of decision making. In the chapters that follow, I want to further explore this model and the implications it holds for anarchist organising and for the idea of anarchist cybernetics. I will do so by returning to Norbert Wiener's original expression of cybernetics as the science of control and communication. By focusing on these two aspects of cybernetics in turn (control in Chapters 4 and 5 and communication in Chapters 6 and 7), I hope to shed light on how anarchist cybernetics can help identify and respond to some of the central issues at the heart of anarchist organising.

4

Control (Part I): Tactics, Strategy and Grand Strategy

If Stafford Beer's Viable Systems Model (VSM) is at the heart of how we might understand organisation from the perspective of an anarchist cybernetics, this has implications for some of the key themes of anarchist and radical left organising. Over the next two chapters, I want to explore these implications in more detail, focusing in this chapter on one possible way of elaborating on the idea of functional hierarchy and what that would then mean for different levels of thinking about anarchist organisation. A sticking point in anarchist theory and practice, at least since the alterglobalisation movement's prominence around the turn of the millennium, has been whether the concept of strategy can be applied to anarchism or whether anarchism is, or ought to be in principle, purely tactical. One of the insights that cybernetics, and specifically the VSM, can provide for us with respect to anarchist organising, I want to argue here, is that the relationship between strategy and tactics can be framed and articulated in such a way as to be wholly consistent with the ideals of self-organisation and participatory democracy that animate anarchism. Moreover, looking at anarchist organisation through the prism of the VSM, we can identify the potential efficacy of considering a further layer over and above tactics and strategy that I refer to in this chapter as 'grand strategy'. For each of these functionally distinct levels – tactics, strategy and grand strategy – I will show how they both contribute to the effectiveness of organisation and at the same time adhere to what we commonly understand as the underlying principles of anarchist organising. Expanding on the concept of functional hierarchy, this chapter discusses how functionally distinct levels of decision making can operate in anarchist organisation.

System and metasystem in the VSM

In the previous chapter, I characterised Beer's VSM as broadly being constituted of two sections. One the one hand, there is the section of the model concerned with the operational parts of the system or organisation, that each possess a level of autonomy with respect to how they go about their business (Systems One and Two). On the other hand, there is the section that deals with bringing those autonomous parts into an overall coherence, in such a way that they can be considered parts of the same system or organisation (Systems Three, Four and Five). Without this second part, Beer argues, the operational units of the first part would simply 'hunt about aimlessly' ([1981] 1994: 129) rather than having any kind of common direction that informs and guides their behaviour. Functionally speaking, the lower autonomous parts of the system or organisation need the higher parts for *metasystemic guidance*. That is, the existence of a system or organisation in any real sense depends on Systems One and Two recognizing, in Beer's words (referring to the parts of a firm), 'that [their] own autonomous division is part of a corporation' ([1981] 1994: 179). That is, Systems One and Two are brought together within a single organisation. Applying this thinking to how anarchist organisation is commonly structured, the various structures of Occupy Wall Street again provide a useful example: the division drawn between lower autonomous operational parts and the higher parts that connect them through providing overall systemic guidance was reflected in and highlighted by the functional roles of working groups in the first or lower section and the general assembly and, later, the spokes council in the second or higher section. In anarchist organisation, whenever individuals come together to discuss the activities taking place in different parts of the organisation and how they contribute to the organisation achieving its goals or even just continuing to exist, they are performing the metasystemic function of the second, higher section of organisation identified by the VSM. As the previous chapter made clear, this functional division does not necessitate a structural division whereby some are excluded from this level of decision making and merely subject to its rule.

Beer stresses the *functional* nature of the division between higher and lower sections in the VSM. He writes, for instance, that '[t]he "higher" level is characterised not by its capacity to command, but by its order of perception and its order of language in logic.' When he speaks of the higher parts of the VSM as constituting a metasystem, he makes clear that meta 'means "over and beyond", referring to the perception and the logic, and not to Seniority' ([1979] 1994: 68–9). It is this recognition, of the importance of such divisions as lying in their functions rather than necessarily concerning positions of hierarchy (as 'seniority'), that creates the possibility for anarchist cybernetics and for an anarchist framing of the VSM. This provides, however, only an overly simplistic and generalised sketch of how functional hierarchy might be applied to an understanding of anarchist organisation. The first step in examining the potential application of such thinking in more detail is an exploration of precisely how the relationship between functionally higher and lower sections of an anarchist organisation might operate, and through doing so considering how genuinely democratic participation at different levels can be facilitated. Thinking about these issues through the more common framework of tactics and strategy provides one useful way of going about this.

In describing the VSM, Beer breaks down the broad distinction, between lower and higher sections of the system, in a way that can help us grasp exactly what is involved in the strategic function of the higher section of the system or organisation. He explains that System Three is concerned with the 'inside and now' of the organisation and System Four with the 'outside and then' ([1979] 1994). This mirrors how strategy is defined by scholars of organisation theory (for example, Carter et al., 2008), whereby strategy is concerned with both what is happening in the moment inside the organisation and how best to regulate it to achieve set goals as well as what is happening outside in the external environment and with respect to the possible futures of the organisation. Thinking about tactics and strategy in the way cybernetics and the VSM encourages is also reflected in how they are conceived of in military contexts. With respect to their military understandings and applications, Carl von Clausewitz ([1832] 1997) defines tactics as that which focuses on specific engagements and strategy as that which brings those engagements together in working towards a common goal. In fact, the kind of autonomy enjoyed by functionally lower sections of the system or organisation in the VSM is not alien to this relationship between strategy and tactics in the military, with the US Marine Crops, for example, operating a notion of 'Mission Tactics', whereby a mission is assigned (strategy) but those completing it have autonomy in deciding how to go about doing that (tactics). Of course, this example clashes with how anarchists understand autonomy as it concerns a *functional* hierarchy operating within a *structurally* hierarchical context. The distinction between what is tactical and what is strategic, however, can be understood in each context in a very similar way (see also Howard Caygill's (2013) work on how Von Clausewitz's thinking can be applied to radical social movements).

Tactics and strategy in anarchist politics

In exploring how tactics and strategy operate in anarchism, the concept of repertoires of action can be useful. In a social movement context, the idea of repertoires was introduced by Charles Tilly (for example, 2010; see also della Porta and Diani, 2006) and refers to how individuals involved in social movements in one way or another come together to take collective action and to the forms that collective action takes. In his book *Anarchy Alive!*, which focused on the varieties of anarchism at work in recent social movements, Uri Gordon applies this concept of repertoires to anarchist politics. 'In terms of action repertoires,' he writes, 'anarchist political culture emphasises a "Do it Yourself" approach of direct action – action without intermediaries, whereby an individual or a group uses their own power and resources to change reality in a desired direction' (2008: 17; see also Franks, 2003, and Graeber, 2009, on direct action and anarchism). For anarchism, then, the kind of repertoires of action that are of interest are those that aim at changing reality in the here and now, at creating alternatives to what presently exists and, where judged to be necessary, directly challenging the dominance or even existence of what exists. In relation to capitalism, for example, the kind of repertoires Gordon and other anarchists are committed to are those that allow people to come together to collectively resist capitalist forms of exchange and replace them with those rooted in concepts such as mutual aid. Importantly, what such anarchists are opposed to is replaced immediately; so that, to stick with the same example, instead of aiming for the creation of a non-capitalist alternative at some point in the future, the goal is realising this alternative in the present, through the repertoire, through the tactical action, itself.

The example of tactical repertoires that try to challenge and replace capitalism sits at the more dramatic or extreme end of what this concept covers. If we think about how repertoires describe the actions that individuals take when they come together in collective forms of organisation, the range of examples within this category runs from the dramatic to the mundane. At one end of this spectrum, there are actions like creating alternatives to capitalism; for instance, through a group setting themselves up as a commune that pools and shares resources based on the maxim of 'from each according to their ability, to each according to their need'. At the other end of the spectrum, there are actions such as cooking a meal. This example might seem out of place, when the intention is to focus on the repertoires and tactics of anarchist social movements, but insofar as mundane actions like cooking a meal together are embedded in and embody particular political frameworks, they can be usefully be considered through this theoretical lens. Cooking a meal, as a collective action, involves decisions about managing resources, divisions of labour, the inclusion of diverse needs and environmental impact, to name but a few of the relevant dimensions to be considered. In this respect, something as apparently simple as a group cooking a meal together is profoundly political and is often bound up with considerations of gender politics as they involve decisions concerning who performs the social reproductive labour required. Anarchist tactical repertoires span the full range of collective actions, from the mundane to the dramatic, that such movements and groups engage in.

If the tactics of anarchist organising cover this range of collective actions that, in one way or another, enact the ideals of anarchist politics – a concept called 'prefiguration', that I will return to later in this chapter – what then is the role of strategy and how does this connect with how I have framed strategy in the context of an anarchist version of the VSM? In this regard, strategy should function in three ways. First, strategy should operate to frame tactical action within the overall goals of the organisation. Second, strategy should be informed by the anarchist politics of self-organisation and participatory democracy discussed throughout this book so far. Third, strategy should be flexible and responsive to change. In the rest of this chapter I want to explore these three functions of strategy.

As discussed previously, in the language of Beer's cybernetics and the VSM, the strategic function in an organisation is concerned with regulating the overall behaviour of the organisation in line with defined goals and in response to change both inside and outside the organisation. This conception of strategy involves a higher function taking place in one (functionally higher) section of the organisation, shaping the semi-autonomous behaviour and functions of other (functionally lower) section of the organisation. This can operate in a number of ways. Strategy can, for example, provide an overarching framework of goals and appropriate tactics which working groups, or other parts of an overall organisation with similar functions of day to day practice, can then fill in, so to speak, in their own ways according to their specific needs, conditions and contexts. This approach is common among recent mobilisations against climate change under the Extinction Rebellion banner, where the organisation has a set of rules and provides resources and general direction, but individual branches decide for themselves how to put these into practice. UK Uncut, a movement of the early 2010s against austerity, similarly relied on a strategy of easily replicable actions that could be crafted to local circumstances. These are not examples of explicitly anarchist organising, but they serve to illustrate how strategy can function in a way that preserves a level of autonomy in the operational parts of an organisation or system while providing guidance that directs these autonomous actions towards set goals (in the next chapter I return to this topic, to further explore this idea of restricted autonomy and discuss how it relates to anarchist discussions of freedom). Strategy is designed to leave enough room for considerable tactical autonomy while functioning to ensure that the exercise of this autonomy contributes towards the overall goals of the organisation.

As well as framing and shaping tactical choices – and the implied possibility, in doing so, of sanctioning or otherwise regulating tactics that diverge from the organisation's overarching goals – strategy also plays a role in determining the structures, mechanisms and processes that are in place in an organisation and how these function both to facilitate autonomy at functionally lower levels of action and democratic participation in all parts of the organisation, including functionally higher ones. As the previous chapter argued, Occupy Wall Street provides an example of one of the ways in which an organisation can be structured to reflect both the anarchist commitment to participation and democracy and the functional requirements identified in Beer's VSM. For the working groups in the camp, the situation was similar to that of Extinction Rebellion groups, in that they possessed a degree of autonomy to make their own choices, but only to the extent these choices were in line with the goals set by functionally higher levels of decision making in the organisation. There is however an important distinction to be drawn between these two examples, one that makes Occupy Wall Street a more apposite case for a discussion of anarchist organisation. With respect to Occupy Wall Street, and in contrast to Extinction Rebellion, the overarching strategy included a structural framework that was aimed at extending participation and democracy throughout the organisation, which included applying these principles of participatory democracy to decisions concerning strategy, in so far as Systems Three and Four strategic functions were conducted by the general assembly and spokes council.

Another way in which we can appreciate the importance of this strategic function in anarchist and radial left organisation is through exploring situations where a distinct lack of strategy is evident in organisations. While I have chosen to use Occupy Wall Street here, as an example of how anarchist organisation can be understood through the lens of the VSM, one of the problems Occupy as a whole and the Wall Street camp specifically faced was a lack of or even resistance to strategic thinking (see Bray, 2013). In such situations, as Beer's description of the role of higher functions in the VSM would suggest, organisations cease to operate effectively as coherent wholes, as the various parts of the organisation instead act independently, without any overarching goals to direct them. At best, the different parts may be able to function as sub-organisations in their own right, setting their own goals and performing strategic functions at a smaller scale, but at worst these units will themselves fall apart and fail to fulfil the basic functions of an organisation. Marianne Maeckelbergh, in her book *The Will of the Many: How the Alterglobalization Movement is Changing the Face of Democracy*, points out how much of the work that has motivated social movements since the 1960s, as well as academic studies of these movements, has prioritised tactics over strategy (Maeckelbergh, 2009). Barbara Epstein (2001) is scathing of this turn in social movements away from strategy and towards what she identifies as a focus on morally charged expression rather than achieving anything. 'What is important', she writes, 'is whether the movement establishes an image of expressing rage for its own sake, or of acting according to an ethical vision.' Maeckelbergh, however, argues that this desire for ethical action is in fact consistent with strategic thinking, if we understand strategy in terms of prefiguration.

Prefiguration

The discussion of the relationship between tactics and strategy covered thus far has centred on what I highlighted as the first dynamic of strategy according to anarchist cybernetics, that strategy provides a guiding framework within which tactical action can be shaped to achieve the goals of the organisation. In this section and the one that follows I want to focus in more detail on the second dynamic of strategy within anarchist cybernetics, that strategy should be open to the participatory democratic self-organisation that is central to anarchist organisation. The concept that is pivotal to this dynamic of strategy is that of prefiguration. Maeckelbergh, drawing on extensive participation in the alterglobalisation movement, provides the following by way of a definition of prefiguration:

> In my experience as an activist, practising prefiguration has meant always trying to make the process we use to achieve our immediate goals an embodiment of our ultimate goals, so that there is no distinction between how we fight and what we fight for, at least not where the ultimate goals of a radically different society is concerned. In this sense, practising prefigurative politics means removing the temporal distinction between the struggle in the *present* towards a goal in the *future*; instead the struggle and the goal, the real and the ideal, become one in the present. (Maeckelbergh, 2009: 66–7, emphasis in original)

Although the term itself was only coined in the 1970s (Boggs, 1977; see also Rowbotham, 1979; Breines, 1980), the practice of prefiguration has a rich history that is, to cite some of the most prominent recent examples, evidenced in the alterglobalisation movement, the horizontalist movement in Argentina (Sitrin and Azzellini, 2014) and the Zapatisa rebellion in Chiapas (Holloway, 2011). It is often summed up by reference to the Industrial Workers of the World slogan 'building a new world in the shell of the old' and its origins are to be found in the anarchist tradition from the late 19th century onwards.

The First International, the attempt in the mid-1860s to bring together a range of left-wing groups across the world, fell apart because of a conflict between those who followed Karl Marx and argued that taking over government and seizing state power are central to building communism and the anarchists who sided with Mikhail Bakunin and his belief that revolution could only come about by building the desired future society in the present. In short, the anarchists in the First International challenged the Marxist strategy of creating political parties to take control of the state in the future, through their own proposals for *prefigurative* strategy that involved enacting anarchism in the here and now. The Jura Federation, the Swiss anarchist grouping that was influenced by Bakunin and that broke with the Marxists in the First International, described this approach to social change as follows:

> The future society should be nothing else than the universalisation of the organisation that the International has formed for itself. We must therefore strive to make this organisation as close as possible to our ideal. How

could we expect an egalitarian and free society to emerge out of an authoritarian organisation! It is impossible. The International, embryo of the future human society, must be, from now on, the faithful image of our principles of liberty and federation, and must reject from within any principle tending toward authority, toward dictatorship. (The Jura Federation, quoted in Gordon, 2018: 528–9)

Emma Goldman (1924), another influential early anarchist theorist and activist, similarly argued that 'methods and means cannot be separated from the ultimate aim. The means deployed become, through individual habit and social practice, part and parcel of the final purpose; they influence it, modify it, and presently the aims and means become identical.'

This identification of means with ends is crucial to prefiguration, and involves an understanding that the political actions we take ought to mirror the goals that we want to achieve. If we want to create, for instance, a future society governed through some form of participatory democracy in which everyone can have a fair say in decision making, then the organisations we build to achieve this should be structured so as to enact that end goal, reflecting it, by themselves focusing on and instigating participatory and democratic forms of decision making. This consideration was a central aspect of the drive behind Occupy's insistence on the kind of democratic processes described in the previous chapter and that I draw on throughout this book. The Occupy camps, not just Occupy Wall Street but others across the world, as well as other mobilisations occurring around the same time such as those of the 15M movement and the Arab Spring, practised this specific form of democracy as providing a microcosm of the kind of society and decision making that they wanted to see extend outside their camps and organisations. Rather than strategising to, for example, create a political party with a typical top-down command and control structure that would stand in elections in the hope of first forming a government and then instigating either a revolution or a set of reforms designed to bring this form of democracy into existence, the prefigurative approach associated with anarchism contends that this democratic goal can only ever be realised by putting it into practice in the ways we organise today and every day. Given what has been described as the electoral turn in contemporary radical politics, reflected in a return to the mass party form by many radical individuals and groups, there is increasing tension on the radical left around the issue of prefigurative strategy, and this is something I will address in the final chapter of this book.

The definition of prefiguration as focused on means (action) embodying or reflecting ends (goals) is shared by a range of authors (for example, Franks, 2006; Maeckelbergh, 2008; Van de Sande, 2013; 2015; Yates, 2014; Gordon; 2018) who approach the concept in theoretical terms and have expanded on it in a range of different ways to account for a number of important considerations, including the temporal ordering of means and ends and the experimental nature of prefigurative action. While there is no space here to discuss these contributions at length, it is possible to offer a definition of prefiguration that draws on them, one that puts the anarchist aim of 'acting as if they are already free' (Graeber, 2009: 433) in more robust and substantive terms. Prefiguration, then, involves:

1. the core desirable features of a future society based on a rejection of domination, exploitation and inequality being realised in the present through
2. alternative structures of power and decision making which involve
3. an equivalence between means and ends that
4. rejects consequentialist approaches that justify means by ends and where
5. both the means and the ends are constantly open for re-articulation.

What this definition captures and foregrounds is that prefiguration is a practice, something that people do, and not just an abstract political concept. As such, while I am primarily applying the concept here in a theoretical or conceptual sense, this does not mean that it exists only, or even primarily, at an abstract level. Indeed, like Beer's VSM, it is as much an attempt at articulating a language to help understand the forms that collective action takes as it is a conceptual framework for proposing how that action ought to look.

Strategy and participation

Maeckelbergh is one of the few authors to explicitly relate the concept and practice of prefiguration to social movement strategy, discussing it as a guide or framework for tactical action:

> [P]refiguration is a movement practice that exists neither instead of strategy nor alongside strategy […] but depending on which type of goal, can be considered to be strategic in itself. […] [I]t constitutes a link between different movement goals and allows for the expression and construction of the

crucially important movement goal of 'another world'.
(Maeckelbergh, 2009: 95)

This account of prefiguration is therefore in stark contrast to that of Epstein and others who have claimed that this prefigurative element of social movements' collective action is only able to account for purely expressive politics. While the prefigurative strategy at work in this kind of action may not reflect how strategy is understood if the primary drivers for political action and organisation are defined in purely consequentialist terms (whereby the correct tactics are those that are judged to make strategic goals more likely to be achieved at some point in the future), prefiguration can still be considered strategic in so far as it provides a framework for understanding how goals can be realised. The key difference between prefigurative and consequentialist politics is that the tactics of prefiguration are intended to enact these desired goals in the present rather than trying to make their realisation more likely in the future. In prefiguration, therefore, the temporal distinction drawn in consequentialist politics between means and ends is removed or collapsed, while the practical distinction between what is considered tactical action and what is strategic decision making is maintained. What does it mean then for strategic decision making in anarchist politics, or indeed for the strategic function of the higher levels of the VSM, to be described as prefigurative?

I want to introduce the idea of 'prefigurative strategy' to help answer this question. Prefigurative strategy concerns how strategic goals in anarchist and radical left organising are developed and agreed on and the way in which these processes of decision making themselves prefigure these goals, at least to the extent that they deal with participatory and democratic forms of governance. As well as the goals or ends of anarchist politics being realised in tactical action that takes place in the immediate present, those goals must also be subject to prefigurative practices of democratic decision making. Indeed, consensus-based decision making and other radically democratic alternative forms of governance are some of the core examples used when authors discuss prefiguration. These prefigurative practices for decision making must be capable of subjecting decisions regarding goals (including the goal of realising these practices) to the same kind of reflection and deliberation that any other form of action would be subject to. Returning to the example of Occupy Wall Street helps illustrate this; a forum, such as the general assembly – which as I suggested earlier performs the strategic function identified by the VSM – must be able to reflect on its own decision-making processes, alongside reflection on the other goals of the camp as a whole, in so far as these processes themselves are both central goals of the politics of the camp as well as a key component of the practices that aim to realise these goals. Linking this back to Beer's cybernetics, Andrew Pickering, in discussing Beer and his work, highlights the concept of the 'purposeful' organisation as one that 'can deliberate on its own ends' (2010: 262). For Beer, organisations, understood cybernetically, are both goal-directed and goal-forming. Prefigurative strategy provides a way of understanding how this goal-forming function can be realised in anarchist organisation and how prefigurative politics differs from more consequentialist accounts, with respect to its understandings of the relationship between tactics and strategy.

Prefigurative strategy, then, is the overall framing that shapes the autonomy that functionally lower units in an organisation have in making tactical choices. Both tactics and strategy prefigure the goals of the organisation; the former through embodying those goals in actions taken, the latter through subjecting the organisation's goals to participatory and democratic reflection and deliberation. In keeping with anarchist cybernetics' resistance to mirroring this type of *functional* hierarchy in a *structurally* hierarchical organisational form, the higher-level *strategic* functions are performed by the same people and groups that take functionally lower *tactical* action. In this way, not only does such anarchist organisation eschew a tactics-only approach to politics, it also avoids creating a structural barrier between the tactical and the strategic which would carry with it the risks of facilitating both the rise of a strategic elite within the organisation and a consequentialist attitude that judges actions in accordance with goals to be achieved in the future rather than goals to be realised in the present. Beer tends towards this line of thinking when he argues that '[i]n order to maintain viability, the total system must have a central regulatory model.' Perhaps this 'central regulatory model' can be understood in terms of the kind of prefigurative strategy just discussed. 'This model', he goes on, 'ought to be created by democratic consultation [...]'. And, noting how tactical constraint can function consistently with democratic control: '[b]ut the vital distinction comes here. The precise form of variety attenuation is a matter for local decision' (1974: 79).

Experimentation, flexibility and adaptation

Something central to the definition of prefiguration offered earlier in this chapter is its experimental nature. Prefiguration, as well as dealing with a mirroring of means and ends, of the actions we take in the present and the goals they aim to realise, is also an ongoing process whereby the tactical repertoires adopted by collective actors are in a continual state of flux and are open to renegotiation over time and across changing circumstances and contexts. This is captured in the prefigurative approach to strategy, whereby the strategic framework that shapes tactical choices is turned back on itself in a critically self-reflective manner, that involves an ongoing process of questioning this framework and overall organisational strategy through the decision-making procedures of the organisation. This constant state of change is perhaps best articulated, however, through the experimental element of prefigurative action. Mathijs van de Sande, writing of the prefigurative politics at work in Tahrir Square in Egypt during the Arab Spring, argues that the space the revolutionaries created there was 'inevitably experimental: it was a moment in which new political ideals could be formulated, realised, tested, improvised and continuously discussed' (2013: 236). This is a common feature in how Van de Sande characterises prefiguration (indeed, he is one of the few authors to highlight this aspect of movement strategy and action) and elsewhere he puts it in the following words:

> In anarchist theory, prefiguration is often presented as a strategy of direct confrontation with the many forms of injustice, repression, and exploitation that characterize the capitalist order. This means in practice that the radical inversion of such relations and forms of repression entails the hypothetical formulation of alternatives and their continuous reformulation through 'trial and error.' The famous Zapatista slogan 'Preguntando caminamos' (or, 'Asking, we walk') perfectly illustrates such an experimental view on radical political processes. (Van de Sande, 2015: 189)

This experimental side of prefiguration, where actions and ideals are, in Van de Sande's words, 'formulated, realized, tested, improvised, and discussed' (2015: 190), can be seen as another point of overlap with Beer's cybernetics, specifically with how he describes the planning function in an organisation. For Beer, planning is the core strategic function of organisations, and in line with his VSM and how strategy brings the various parts of the organisation or system into a coherent whole, planning is considered the 'glue' that holds the organisation together. How planning is understood from Beer's perspective, however, is not how we might typically think of a plan – that is, as something drawn up prior to a particular course of action and then implemented as a set of rules to follow. For Beer, planning is instead a 'continuous process' ([1979] 1994: 336) and his approach to planning hints at something of a prefigurative attitude: '[p]lanning is *not* an activity resulting in products called plans: it is a continuous process, whereby the process itself – namely that of aborting the plans – is the pay-off' [1979] 1994: 338, emphasis in original). The goals that are developed in the planning process are, therefore, constantly aborted and rearticulated as both the organisation and its environment change. Andrew Pickering describes this line of thinking in Beer's work as 'adaptive' (2010: 224), because the planning process is about strategies that adapt to change through assessing a situation, introducing goals and relevant tactics, reassessing as things change, and abandoning those goals and tactics for new ones in an ongoing cycle.

This continual strategic process of aborting plans and devising new ones as organisations and their environments change is a feature that organisational cybernetics and prefigurative politics share in common. The 'endless flux of planning processes' that Beer emphasises can be recognised in the experimental and flexible nature of this kind of political organisation and action, where prefiguration, and in particular its application to strategy, is central. Not only does prefiguration entail a participatory and democratic approach to proposing, agreeing and achieving strategic goals, but these goals are also experimental, being reassessed continually. In a similar manner, tactical repertoires are developed, applied, assessed and abandoned in an ongoing cycle. Much like how Walter understood self-organisation at work in his tortoise robots (as I discussed in the previous chapter), prefigurative organising is also constantly rearticulating its direction towards goals that are constantly shifting. Where anarchist self-organisation differs from that described by Walter is that it is both goal-seeking *and* goal-making through processes of democratic participation.

Grand strategy

The characterisation of the relationship between strategy and tactics in anarchist cybernetics just outlined raises a potentially important sticking point. On the face of it, this idea, that strategic goals should be decided on in a way that prefigures the goals of the organisation, seems to be circular. How can goals be decided on in a way that prefigures these very goals? Of course, once one set of goals is in place, other goals can be agreed on through processes that prefigure the original goals, thus creating new sets of goals. And as long as new goals are reached in ways that reflect decision making ideals (such as participatory democracy), then the original set of goals can even be abandoned in line with the need, outlined in the previous section, for strategy to be flexible and experimental in nature. For example, an organisation could begin with a set of goals that included enacting democracy through respecting the will of the majority of the participants. Using this decision-making procedure, the organisation could then reassess this goal and alter it to reflect an ideal of democracy based on consensus (by achieving majority support for the shift to consensus based decision making). They would have thus prefigured their ideal practice of democracy to reassess this ideal and abandon it in favour of another ideal. This cycle might continue, with the ideal of consensus decision making being reassessed and abandoned to be replaced by modified consensus, where if full consensus is not achievable a super-majority of 90 per cent approval is deemed acceptable (more on this in the next chapter). This might look like a perfectly decent way for strategy to operate in a prefigurative manner, but if we look back to the start of the cycle there is a potential problem. How is the very first set of goals decided on? If there are no goals in place to prefigure, how can any goal-making be prefigurative?

If it is assumed that this is then a problem for the strategic prefigurative aspect of anarchist cybernetics I am presenting here, where might we find a solution? Throughout this chapter, I have suggested that we identify the strategic function in an organisation with the functionally higher levels of the VSM, but I have thus far only discussed Systems Three and Four. To find a solution to the potential problem of the first goals of anarchist organisation, we need to look at System Five. While it is true to say that the functionally higher part of the VSM, made up of Systems Three, Four and Five, are where strategic functions are located, it is strictly speaking incorrect to group these three sub-systems together as performing a single function. As I noted earlier in this chapter, Systems Three and Four are charged with strategic decision making with respect to what happens both outside and inside the organisation as well as both in the present and in the predicted future, with these functions being initially housed in the general assembly of the Occupy camps and later, at least in Occupy Wall Street, in the spokes council. What role then is played by System Five? In the VSM, System Five sits at the top of the model, but in applying such terminological representation ('the top'/'higher'/'lower' and so on) across the model as a whole, this should not be seen as denoting a *structural* authority or hierarchy, with an elite at the top. It does, however, signal a strategic *functional* authority over decision making at functionally lower levels in the organisation. Beer describes the function of System Five as providing an overarching ethos, normative planning or identity for the organisation ([1979] 1994: 354). System Five contains, in a sense, the worldview or paradigm of the organisation.

If we take radical left organisation in general as an example, it is easy to see what this paradigm function might involve. Maeckelbergh, for instance, highlights the 'ultimate goal' of radical movements as 'overthrowing capitalism' and 'to create a world in which people are empowered to collectively set their own agendas and pursue their own aims' (2009: 94; 13). Jenny Pickerill and Paul Chatterton identify a 'common sense' of the alterglobalisation movement in these overarching goals, that served to shape the various forms of action that movement actors collectively took (2006: 735). David Graeber, in his discussion of Occupy Wall Street, similarly points towards the identity of the organisation in its 'We are the 99%' meme, understood as a form of ideology (2013: 84). How do these examples of this highest level of the strategy function in these organisations, however, help us appreciate ways to overcome the problem of an original set of goals designed to kick-start the prefigurative strategic cycle? Luke Yates makes the interesting comment in his discussion of prefiguration that there are 'realisable, negotiable, targeted and precise movement goals, as well as some that [are] overarching and non-negotiable' (2014: 16; see also Mueller: 2003). For anarchism, then, we might say that there exists an anti-capitalist, anti-domination worldview that determines the parameters for possible strategies and, in turn, possible tactics, but that this worldview is not as flexible or open to experiment and change as strategy is. In cybernetic terminology, while Systems Three and Four perform a strategic function that is open to change through participatory and democratic decision making, System Five performs a far more fundamental function – in that it provides the initial goals or worldview that originate the prefigurative strategic cycle, goals that are considerably less open to change.

That some aspects of anarchist organisation are less open to change than others may sound controversial in relation to how anarchist cybernetics has been discussed thus far, as having participatory and democratic self-organisation at its heart, but it is in fact something very common across radical and anarchist forms of organisation. The unchangeable (or at least not easily changeable) paradigm or worldview represents a sine qua non ('without which not') of such organisations: without these goals, they would not be that kind of organisation, their core identity would be altered. When understood in these terms, this function can be seen, for instance, in the opposition to fascism as being the sine qua non of Anti-Fascist Action and similar groups, or in the rejection of all forms of economic exploitation of radical trade unions like the Industrial Workers of the World. If such organisations decided to stop being opposed to fascism or economic exploitation, they would no longer be the same organisations. These fundamental sets of principles are, therefore, difficult if not impossible to challenge within these organisations. If a member or participant sought to change them, they would perhaps be better advised to look for a different organisation to join. In the case of the Industrial Workers of the World, for instance, the Preamble to the Constitution, which states that 'the working class and the employing class have nothing in common', has remained unchanged in any substantial way since 1905. This does not mean that the organisation's strategies and tactics have not changed as social and economic conditions have developed over time, but that the overarching principles and goals that shape these strategies and tactics are the same as they were over a century ago.

I want to refer to this highest functional level in the VSM and in anarchist organisation as 'grand strategy' (Vanilla Beer and Allenna Leonard use the term 'norms' to distinguish System Five (Beer and Leonard, 2019)). This term was coined by the US military theorist John Boyd during the Cold War. Boyd was inspired by Norbert Wiener's work on complexity (see Freedman, 2013) and provided his ideas on strategy and grand strategy in a large set of presentation slides rather than in essays or books, and it is to these slides that I refer here. While Boyd defines grand strategy in military terms befitting of the Cold War era, a more general appreciation of the concept and exploration of how it relates to strategy and tactics is useful for helping articulate the functional role of System Five in the VSM. Boyd speaks of grand strategy as a 'unifying vision': 'A grand ideal, overarching theme, or a noble philosophy that represents a coherent paradigm within which individuals as well as societies can shape and adapt to unfolding circumstances – yet offers a way to expose flaws of competing or adversary systems' (Boyd, 2005: slide 144).

This reflects the way in which a worldview or paradigm functions in an anarchist cybernetics' understanding of anarchist organisation. Indeed, this statement on grand strategy mirrors how social movements scholar Darcy Leach defines ideology:

> a collectively held system of beliefs, subjectively taken to be true, which incorporates a theory of how society works, a set of values about the end-states and principles of behaviour that should govern society, and a set of attitudes

about people, objects, issues, and practices that correspond to those values. (Leach, 2009: 1050)

In the context of this discussion, grand strategy includes content concerning the overarching end-goals of anarchist politics but also, as with Leach's comment on ideology, the framework that defines actors and repertoires while reflecting the principles or values contained in those end-goals. Grand strategy, as Boyd defines it, shows how this function can be understood as also responding to what he calls 'unfolding circumstances' or the kind of complexity and change discussed in this book. Boyd's inclusion of 'a way to expose the flaws of competing or adversary systems' is similarly important in that it highlights, with regard to an anarchist and radical left context, how critiques of both capitalism and different forms of domination and exploitation shape the strategies and tactics that organisations adopt. For example, returning to the Industrial Workers of the World, that organisation's focus on workplace organising comes from its analysis of work as the main point at which capitalism operates as a system of exploitation and at which it can be resisted by exerting control over the process of production. Other organisations, with other critiques (identifying other sites of domination and oppression), will have other corresponding sets of strategies and tactics for resistance and the provision of alternatives in their repertoires. What is important when it comes to grand strategy as the function of System Five in the VSM is that they provide the overarching principles and goals that make strategic decision making and, downstream from that, tactical action, possible within a single coherent organisational agenda. As Beer writes of System Five, this function 'provides implied answers to the questions people are asking' ([1979] 1994: 354). In deciding what strategies are appropriate and what tactical action collectives can and should take, the grand strategy of System Five provides the guidance needed to make such decisions.

The addition of the spokes-council to Occupy Wall Street can be viewed as illustrating an attempt to more clearly separate the (functionally higher) grand strategic function of System Five from the (functionally lower) general strategic functions of Systems Three and Four. At the general assembly where the spokes-council model was proposed and agreed on, one participant (quoted in Kinna et al., 2019: 376) argued that the spokes-council 'would deal with logistical and financial decisions, whereas the [general assembly] would deal with larger political questions about OWS and the greater movement'. This provides a clear statement of the distinction between these two functionally separate levels of decision making. The spokes-council, which included delegates from working groups and caucuses mandated by their groups to support certain agreements, dealt with general (rather than grand) strategic matters such as finance and logistics, which would then have an impact on the tactical choices that were open to the working groups. The general assembly, where all participants could be part of the decision-making process, would maintain the grand strategic function of debating the movements aims and identity, its overarching goals and fundamental principles. As Keir Milburn notes (2019), the general assembly also played the role of allowing individuals to express themselves within the collective, including providing the opportunity for participants to identify themselves within the overarching narrative of, in the case of Occupy, the 99%. Again, this role fits within the conception of the general assembly as possessing a grand strategic function. Graham Jones, inspired by Beer's cybernetics, makes a similar point as to distinguishing between different types of strategic movement (or as he calls it, ecology) functions such as 'collecting the information that allows the assemblies to make decisions on strategy' (a System Four strategic function in the VSM) and 'decisions affecting future-orientation such as realigning the ecology's short-, medium- and long-term goals [that] must go to the wider membership' (a System Five grand strategic function) (2018: 112).

While this division of functions across different institutions within Occupy Wall Street was not able to be fully implemented, due to the camp being evicted soon after the spokes-council was initiated, it does illustrate an important development of the Occupy model that anarchist cybernetics can help us to understand.

Conclusion

The aim of this chapter has been to further elaborate on how Beer's Viable System Model operates within the anarchist cybernetics framework that animates the discussions contained in this book. The VSM provides us with three distinct but related functional levels of decision making and acting. Systems One and Two help explain how organisations, or rather the separate parts of organisations such as the working groups of Occupy Wall Street, take collective *tactical* action. Systems Three and Four articulate the *strategic* decision making that frames such tactical action within the overall goals of the organisation, that in Occupy can be seen in the function played initially by the general assembly and later by the spokes council. System Five, in turn, highlights the *grand strategic* function, played by the general assembly in

Occupy, which operates on a functionally different (higher) level to that making the decisions relevant to general strategic functions (Systems Three and Four). This final level, of grand strategy formulation, involves the establishment and development of the overarching worldview or paradigm within which both strategy and tactics are framed. Grand strategy, I have shown, refers to the end-goals and fundamental principles of the organisation that provide it with an identity and which are difficult, if not often impossible, to change. In contrast, strategy is in a constant state of flux, reflected in how the idea of strategy in these contexts is informed by the flexible and experimental nature of prefigurative politics. In the next chapter, I want to turn to what this schema means for autonomy in anarchist cybernetics. Anarchism is often taken to indicate a commitment to individual and collective autonomy. As well as exploring what this means in practice, the next chapter will also suggest how strategic constraints on tactical autonomy are in fact consistent with anarchist politics.

5

Control (Part II): Effective Freedom and Collective Autonomy

Autonomy is one of the most central ideas in both anarchist political theory and in cybernetics. For the former, autonomy provides one of the key motivations that drives political practice. For the latter, it represents the fundamental condition required for a system's survival. While the same terminology is used in both literatures, in this chapter I want to suggest that there are in fact two distinct but connected definitions of autonomy at play − *Functional Autonomy*, drawn from cybernetics, and *Collective Autonomy*, developed through a reading of anarchism and related social movement traditions. These reflect two different sides of anarchist cybernetics: the ethical or political side, that champions anarchy and autonomy because they entail the freedoms individuals and groups are entitled to; and the practical side, that proclaims anarchy as the most effective way to structure a complex society. This chapter will also attempt to show how anarchism reconciles individual and collective autonomy, focusing on how the much-maligned practice of consensus decision making is vital in this regard. I begin the discussion with an overview of the role played by the idea of autonomy in cybernetics.

Autonomy in organisational cybernetics

In her book on Beer's attempt at putting organisational cybernetics into practice in Salvador Allende's Chile in the early 1970s, Eden Medina writes that 'cybernetic management approached the control problem in a way that preserved a degree of freedom and autonomy for the parts without sacrificing the stability of the whole' (2011: 29). As discussed in the previous two chapters, this idea of balance, between autonomy on the one hand, and centralisation on the other, is crucial, both with respect to both Beer's cybernetics and with regard to its manifestation in anarchist cybernetics (Duda, 2012). While autonomy is essential for an organisation to be able to flexibly react and respond to complexity and change, at the same time, some degree of coherence between autonomous parts is just as important, because otherwise there would be no organisation, with overarching goals, to speak of. Just as Beer argues that the operational units of any organisation should enjoy a high level of autonomy, he also insists that they should be subject to what he describes as 'managerial constraint'. In *Brain of the Firm*, the book in which he did the most to introduce and outline the key principles behind his cybernetics, he identified three such constraints ([1981] 1994: 158–62):

1. autonomous parts must operate in coordination with other autonomous parts;
2. autonomous parts must operate within the intentions of the whole organisation; and
3. autonomous parts must face the possibility of being excluded from the organisation as a whole.

These three restrictions on autonomy reflect, for Beer, the fact that any individual part of an organisation can '"do what it likes" within just one limitation: it continues to belong' ([1981] 1994: 159). Let's take these constraints in turn and look at what each of them means for organisation.

The first of these constraints on autonomy is that the operational parts of the organisation need to recognise that other parts exist within the same organisation and that coordination with these other parts is essential. As Beer puts it, there must be a *'co-ordinating framework'* ([1981] 1994: 160, emphasis in original) that connects the individual parts of the organisation, restricting autonomy so that the actions of one part do not impact negatively on the actions of others. For Beer, the key to facilitating this coordination is an effective communication network between different parts of the organisation. Important for understanding the restriction of autonomy this involves, as encapsulated by the System Two functions in the Viable System Model (VSM), is that at this level coordination does not mean cooperation. The separate units of the organisation may coordinate so that their actions do not impinge on those of other units, identifying and maintaining borders between each unit's niche, but they do not discuss and agree on common goals and determine how best to work together towards those goals. That is a function for functionally higher levels of the organisation, and it is at these levels that the second and third constraints on autonomy come into play.

The second constraint on autonomy, for Beer, is the condition that the autonomous parts of the organisation need to work '*within the intention of the whole*' ([1981] 1994: 159). This reflects the discussion in the previous chapter concerning the shaping of tactical action in line with the strategic and grand strategic goals of an organisation. These goals, negotiated at functionally higher levels of an organisation, represent constraints on the tactical choices available to functionally lower operating units within the organisation. This is perhaps the most important aspect of how autonomy features in organisational cybernetics because it represents the crucial balance that needs to be struck, between autonomy and centralised cohesion, that allows organisations to be flexible and responsive to change, while maintaining a shared direction that brings the different parts together as one organisation. Crucially, then, tactical autonomy is not the absolute freedom to choose any course of action but, according to organisational cybernetics, is a restricted choice, where the restrictions are determined by functionally higher levels of strategic and grand strategic decision making. Reflecting discussions earlier in this book concerning this balance between tactical autonomy and organisational cohesion, later in this chapter I will attempt to show how maintaining such a balance can be consistent with the participatory and democratic forms of organisation that anarchist cybernetics is concerned with.

The final constraint on autonomy Beer highlights is potentially the most controversial, particularly when we look at how it might figure in anarchist organisation. According to Beer, the individual operating units of the organisation need to face the possibility of the ultimate restriction on their autonomy: they must, so Beer argues, acknowledge not only their presence in an organisational whole with other autonomous parts and with overarching goals that restrict their tactical choices but also the fact that they may be excluded from the organisation. In other words, their autonomy may be restricted to the extent that they are no longer accepted as a part of the organisation and are ejected. This is, in part, about weighing the needs of the many against the needs of the few (something Medina (2011) discusses in relation to cybernetics in Chile) but also considers the survival of the organisation as a whole and as such comes down to questions concerning not only what benefits the whole but what maintains (or potentially threatens) the organisation's very existence. With respect to the contexts that Beer was primarily working within (those of commercial enterprises), this may be generally accepted as part and parcel of the cut and thrust of business, but for any application of cybernetics to anarchist organisation this suggests a potential stumbling block. As with the second restriction on autonomy, however, later in this chapter I aim to demonstrate that this third restriction is also in fact consistent with how autonomy and freedom are conceived of in anarchism, or at least with respect to an important strand of the anarchist tradition.

Functional autonomy

Before exploring how these constraints on autonomy can operate in anarchist cybernetics, it is vital to elaborate a little on precisely what Beer means by autonomy in his organisational cybernetics. Beer's thoughts on autonomy are at their most clear and penetrating in his reflections on his experience in Chile. In 1973 he gave a speech titled 'Fanfare for Effective Freedom. Cybernetics Praxis in Government', in which he stated: 'the polarity between centralisation and decentralisation – one masquerading as oppression and the other as freedom – is a myth' (1973: 6). This understanding is present through his work; even as early as in the 1967 second edition of *Cybernetics and Management,* he wrote of the hard distinction between autonomy and centralised control that 'the [cybernetic] model shows how naïve that dichotomy is as an organisational description. No viable organism is either centralised or decentralised. It is both things at once, in different dimensions.' (Beer, 1967: 75–6).

It is after the fall of Allende's government and the end of Project Cybersyn, however, that he properly elaborates on this aspect of the cybernetic model, defining it as 'effective freedom' and claiming that 'the degree of autonomy, and its complement degree of centralisation, are computable functions of viability' (1973: 16). Such computability suggests a quantifiability of freedom or autonomy, and indeed Medina indeed points out Beer's articulation '(1) that freedom was something that could be calculated and (2) that freedom should be quantitatively circumscribed to ensure the stability of the overall system' (2011: 181). As an aside, the quantitative nature of freedom, as Beer defined it, is perhaps something that is more a part of the performative ontology of second-order cybernetics, as discussed in Chapter 3, and less an essential feature of this more general approach to autonomy. For complexity and variety to be made manageable in processes of organising, the 'truth' of them needs to be constructed in ways that make them operationally useful. This more fluid and less rigorous way of navigating complexity may not require the kind of quantification Beer describes and it might instead be preferable to speak of more or less freedom, rather than specified amounts.

For Beer's cybernetics, therefore, in a similar manner to how hierarchy is characterised in *functional* terms so too is autonomy classed as a function for effective, viable organisation. Autonomy, then, is a purely *descriptive* concept in so far as it identifies a functional condition in the parts of a system or organisation and is only of value in so far as it can be said to contribute to that system or organisation being viable. Indeed, for Beer, the aim of cybernetics is to '*design* autonomy according to cybernetic principles' ([1987] 1994: 19, emphasis in original); the use of autonomy is unrelated to a *normative* conceptualisation that values it for its own sake (that is, that organisations should be structured to enhance autonomy because autonomy is a quality we consider as good). As Beer puts it elsewhere, '[i]f a system regulates itself by subtracting *at all times* as little horizontal variety as is necessary to maintain the cohesion of the total system, then the condition of autonomy prevails' ([1974] 1994: 332, emphasis in original). What this means is, that if only the minimum level of restriction is imposed on autonomous tactical choice that is necessary for the organisation as a whole to function effectively, if the different parts of a system or organisation are only constrained to the minimum level required for organisational cohesion, then functional autonomy can be said to exist. Beyond this, from a purely cybernetics perspective, Beer is not interested in freedom or any normative understanding that values the autonomy of individuals or groups in and of itself.

Of course, in so far as Beer was a progressively minded person, he was concerned with freedom as a political principle. In various texts he discusses topics that we might more commonly consider in relation to questions of political autonomy, such as participatory and democratic decision making ([1981] 1994: 161–2), worker self-management of industry (1972a) and direct forms of parliamentary democracy (1972b). The point here is not that organisational cybernetics demands a rejection of ethical or political formulations of autonomy or freedom but that in the context of cybernetics and the VSM, autonomy is a different concept entirely from how we use the term in ethical or political thinking. As Beer notes, this account of autonomy is 'distinct from the ethical, political, or psychological arguments' on the topic ([1979] 1994: 158). Given such considerations, I want to provide the following definition of autonomy as it can be understood in the context of organisational cybernetics:

> *Functional Autonomy*: the degree of flexibility an individual or group within an organisation has to respond to complexity as they see fit, while remaining within constraints set by their relationship to other groups and individuals in the organisation, the goals of the organisation as a whole and the potential for being expelled from the organisation.

As already discussed, this definition should only be taken to apply to how autonomy operates as a function within a viable system or organisation; it is the minimal necessary and sufficient definition that can be applied to organisational cybernetics as Beer articulates it.

Anarchism and autonomy

Beer is dismissive of what he calls the 'anarchist' view of autonomy, arguing that it is incompatible with the definition of autonomy in organisational cybernetics (1979 [1994]: 156). Considering only the functions of an effective or viable organisation, Beer's belief in the incompatibility of an anarchist conception of autonomy is based on his understanding of such a conception as meaning that any part of the organisation should be able to do whatever it wants, regardless of what this means for other parts of the organisation or indeed for the organisation as a whole. This understanding of autonomy is perhaps best characterised as an extreme form of individualism and given what has been discussed with respect to how effective organisation is understood in Beer's cybernetics, it is unsurprising that he would reject such a view of autonomy. Is Beer right, however, to characterise this as an anarchist position? Is it true to say that the *Functional Autonomy* required by cybernetics and the VSM is antithetical to how anarchists approach the idea of autonomy? Even though an anarchist commitment to autonomy would be situated in the political or normative sphere, rather than the descriptive or functional one that Beer is most interested in, any organisation that championed *Functional Autonomy* as well as a normative or political individualism would be at an impasse. The constraints required by *Functional Autonomy* would be undermined by a political or normative conceptualisation of autonomy that opposed all constraint. How, then, can *Functional Autonomy* be a consistent component of an anarchist cybernetics that genuinely reflects an anarchist account of autonomy and freedom? To answer this fundamental question, I want to look at the different ways in which autonomy has been understood in the anarchist tradition.

The issue of individual autonomy in anarchism has often proved contentious. On the one hand, there is a strong individualist strain running through the anarchist tradition, with anarchists who are commonly associated with collectivist or communist anarchisms espousing what, on the face of it, may seem like highly individualist statements. Mikhail Bakunin, for instance, described himself as a 'fanatical lover of liberty'. He rejected what he called 'individualist, egoist, base, and fraudulent liberty' – associating this with 'bourgeoise liberalism' but nonetheless spoke favourably of 'the liberty which knows no other restrictions but those set by the laws of our own nature'. 'Consequently', he went on, 'there are, properly speaking, no restrictions, since these laws are not imposed on us by any legislator from outside, alongside, or above ourselves' (1871). In a similar vein, Emma Goldman argued that 'the individual is the heart of the society, conserving the essence of social life; society is the lungs which are distributing the element to keep the life essence – that is, the individual – pure and strong' (Goldman, [1910] 1969: 58).

Goldman was partly inspired in her anarchism by Nietzsche (Moore, 2004) and his influence can indeed be seen in this ideal of society as a supporting framework for the individual and their autonomy.

The approach to autonomy reflected here is often more commonly associated with a radical liberalism than with the anarchist tradition (as Bookchin argues, 1995) and can even be identified in the work of some of the earliest proponents of liberal political theory, such as John Stuart Mill, who defined the autonomous individual as one who 'acts according to his [sic] own inclination and judgement in things which concern himself' (1977: 119). The philosopher Gerald Dworkin has similarly characterised the idea of autonomy as 'a notion of the self which is to be respected, left unmanipulated, and which is, in certain ways, independent and self-determining' (1988: 11–12). While these liberal accounts may temper their commitment to individual autonomy through, for example, a conception of legitimate restriction based on the principle of non-maleficence or of doing no harm, placing such an ideal of autonomy at the heart of political theory can also tend towards support for the kind of individualism associated with neoliberal market economics. Social geographers Jenny Pickerill and Paul Chatterton, for instance, link this 'free-floating individual with highly egoistic desires' to 'market interactions between rational, autonomous and self-interested individuals' and to 'modern-day consumer societies' (2006: 733). Of course, the intentions of even some of the most ardently individualist anarchists, such as Max Stirner (1995), would reject this manifestation of autonomy in neoliberal economics, but from the perspective of anarchist cybernetics, there is a clash between an individualist commitment to autonomy and the need for constraint and functional autonomy.

The question of individualism in anarchism is a far from simple topic to cover in the brief space permitted by this chapter. While, for anarchist cybernetics, a position that rejects complete, unrestrained autonomy is clearly a necessity, in the anarchist tradition more broadly there is disagreement around the desirability of restraints on autonomy. The critique of what we might call a liberal form of autonomy finds its roots at least as far back as the work of Peter Kropotkin. In the entry he wrote on anarchism for the *Encyclopaedia Britannica* in 1910 (which was rejected by the publishers), he criticised individualist anarchism because it necessarily entailed an aristocracy, the freedom of which was predicated on the subjugation others. This also meant that such individualism bred contradiction, as the supposed autonomy of all (the professed aim) was, in any realistic application, actually predicated on the domination of others. Kropotkin acknowledged the importance of individual development but maintained that this demanded, in the first instance, collective organisation as the fertile ground in which individual development could then bloom. He wrote that in regard to anarchist organisation the individual 'would thus be enabled to obtain the full development of all his [*sic*] faculties, intellectual, artistic and moral, without being hampered by overwork for the monopolists, or by the servility and inertia of mind of the great number' (Kropotkin, 1910). Importantly, it is collective society that is the starting point from which individual autonomy develops and in which it finds its limits. For Kropotkin, this meant that the individual 'would thus be able to reach full *individualization*, which is not possible either under the present system of *individualism*' (emphasis in original).

Collective autonomy

For anarchists like Kropotkin, therefore, individual autonomy is neither the point of origin of political theory (which would entail all social and political organisation being subservient to the autonomy of the individual) nor is it understood in terms of an unconstrained liberty (whereby any restriction is seen as an injustice). Rather, autonomy is understood as dependent on collective organisation for its development and is thus constrained by this collective setting, its relation to the autonomy of others and the demands of maintaining the collective.

One of the political and activist traditions that has best characterised this form of autonomy is the *Autonome* movement in Germany, which sits adjacent to anarchism. In a way that chimes well with how anarchist cybernetics has been framed thus far in this book, the *Autonomen* articulate autonomy as a property of collectives rather than of individuals. This conception thus also situates the question of autonomy firmly in the context of organisation rather than in the idea of a freely floating individual. The *Autonome* feminist writer and activist Marie-Therese Knapper, for instance, states that '[w]ithin the movement, autonomy means primarily decentralization, autonomy of every single group' (quoted in Katsiaficas, 2001: 549). George Katsiaficas defines autonomy along similar lines, in relation to 'we' rather than 'I' (2006).

The focus on collective rather than individual autonomy does not mean that individuals are subsumed into collective entities and that there is no space in *Autonomen* thinking for individual freedom. The important distinction between this position on autonomy and that of individualist anarchists is that individual autonomy is rejected as the starting point for political organisation. Instead, and largely in tune with Kropotkin's account of autonomy, individual freedom is a product of collective organisation; it issues forth from instances of collectivity where individuals come together and work in co-operation towards collective goals. Prominent *Autonome* activist Geronimo quotes Bobo Schulze on this point, defining autonomy as a property or characteristic of collective organisational relationships:

> 'Autonomy' is a fragile thing. Or rather: autonomy is no thing at all. It stands for a certain form of relationship between people who associate in order to destroy all forms of oppression. It is a relationship that cannot be grasped theoretically. Theories can only be formulated about phenomena that exist in and by themselves. 'Autonomy' only exists when people start to be active revolutionaries. (Schulze, quoted in Geronimo, 2012: 19)

From this perspective, it is only in contexts of collective, revolutionary organisation, therefore, that autonomy can be identified and spoken of at all. Far from being a point of origin for political organisation it is in fact an outcome, one that is impossible without such organisation first being in place.

This distinction is made clear by Katsiaficas in the following passage, in which he eschews what he describes as 'ontological individualism':

> My ontology is that thousands of people acting in
> social movements embody the concrete realization of
> freedom: Outside established norms and institutions,
> thousands of people consciously act spontaneously in concert.
> In such moments [...] genuine individuality emerges as
> human beings situate themselves in collective contexts that
> negate their individualism. (Katsiaficas, 2006: 259)

The ontology here, that is, the belief in how the world and reality is
structured, is one in which collective organisation precedes individual
autonomy or freedom. There is a striking parallel in this regard
with Kropotkin's contrast of individualism with individualisation,
the latter being an account of autonomy that is made possible by
organisation. Pickerill and Chatterton conceive of autonomy in
similar terms: autonomy, they argue, 'is a collective project fulfilled
only through reciprocal and mutually agreed relations with others'
(2006: 733). Indeed, this definition of autonomy harks back to how the
concept was originally used in Ancient Greece. As Dworkin points out,
'autonomia' referred not to individuals but to the city or the polis, the
unit of social and political organisation: '[a] city had *autonomia* when its
citizens made their own laws, as opposed to being under the control
of some conquering power' (1988: 12–13). While this leans too far
towards the extreme collectivism that anarchists oppose – Kropotkin
for instance rejected both liberal individualism and what he called
the 'system of state socialism in the so-called *Volkstaat* (popular state)'
(1910) – it nonetheless highlights the balance required by the ideal
of autonomy at the centre of this discussion; a balance between the
extremes of individualism on the one hand and collectivism on the
other. In her work on the German *Autonomen*, Darcy Leach writes that
autonomy is about 'balancing collective responsibility and solidarity
against the right of self-determination' (2009: 1057).

Drawing on how autonomy is understood by the German *Autonome*
movement and by theorists such as Katsiaficas, it is possible to outline
a conceptualisation of autonomy that both stands in contrast to
the liberal or individualist account and that is compatible with the
needs of anarchist cybernetics. Paraphrasing Charlotte Baarts (2009;
following Gullestad, 1992), I want to call this definition of autonomy
'collective autonomy'. Like Baarts' 'collective individualism', it refers
to a 'negotiation' or 'balancing act' whereby 'the scope of individualism
seems to be defined by the extent of conformity with the standards
of the community and [...] consensus' (Baarts, 2009: 955). It also,
importantly, has the potential to cohere with sociological descriptions

in which individualisation is dependent on social structures (see for instance, the classic work of Georg Simmel (1971)).

Linking this directly to anarchism, David Bell (2014) highlights the role of this collective understanding of individual autonomy by focusing on the practice of musical improvisation, which requires the structure provided by the collective band to make possible and shape the individual freedom expressed by the individual musician. Rather than improvisation allowing for an unrestrained individualism, the individual is instead subject to constraints such as key, scale and timing and is part of a process of negotiation with the collective of musicians. Without these constraints, the individual is limited to performing alone; with them, they are individually empowered and enabled by the collective. This line of thought on autonomy is, for Bookchin, reason to actually reject the term 'autonomy' in favour of 'freedom'. He argues that the word 'autonomy' has its conceptual roots in individualism, something 'freedom', derived from the German *freiheit*, avoids through its connotation of collectivity:

> When applied to the individual, freedom thus preserves a social or collective interpretation of that individual's origins and development as a self. In 'freedom,' individual selfhood does not stand opposed to or apart from the collective but is significantly formed [...] by his or her own social existence. Freedom thus does not subsume the individual's liberty but denotes its actualization. (Bookchin, 1995: 12–13)

This is undoubtedly an important conceptual and terminological point, but because of how autonomy is used in cybernetics and in anarchist-adjacent political movements like the German *Autonomen*, I am going to stick with the word 'autonomy'. As I hope is clear from the discussion thus far, however, I will use it in the way Bookchin believed the word 'freedom' should be used.

In contrast to liberal individualism, then, collective autonomy can be defined as follows:

> *Collective Autonomy* is the collectively determined capacity and scope an individual or group has to decide and act within the constraints set by collective organisation.

This definition of autonomy, one that rejects both the liberal and individualist focus on the autonomous individual subject as the starting point for politics, returns us to how the concept is used in Beer's cybernetics. Earlier in this chapter, I provided an overview of *Functional*

Autonomy, of autonomy or freedom understood as an identifiable function or characteristic of the parts of a viable system or organisation. For Beer, for any organisation to be able to respond to complexity, parts of it must be, to an extent, autonomous. While Beer's *Functional Autonomy* is not intended to refer to what we commonly understand as social or political freedom, the idea of *Collective Autonomy* provides a possible convergence that allows both concepts to inhabit the same image of organisation, even though they articulate different things. Importantly, like *Functional Autonomy*, the notion of *Collective Autonomy* frames the freedom individuals and groups have within the demands of the collective, organisational setting. For *Functional Autonomy*, this organisational framework restricts operational freedom because the various operational parts must ultimately belong to a whole and work towards the goals of that whole. For *Collective Autonomy*, freedom is not possible without a collective or organisational framework and is both conditioned and constrained by this as a necessary element of its existence. So while the two definitions of autonomy offered in this chapter refer to different aspects of how an organisation can be structured and of the role of individuals and groups within such structures, they do not contradict one another. By recognising the necessity of collective organisation for the existence of autonomy, they entail a similar set of conditions within which their different, yet complementary, accounts of autonomy are made possible.

Consensus decision making

If both *Functional Autonomy* and *Collective Autonomy* are defined, in part, as a negotiation between individualism and collectivism, between the desire for operational freedom and the need to remain part of an overarching organisation, what does this mean for the practice of anarchist organisation and for anarchist cybernetics? To address this question, I want to turn to how decision making operates in anarchist organising and to consider decision making procedures as one of the ways in which this negotiation or balancing act can be implemented, both in terms of *Functional Autonomy* and *Collective Autonomy*. While democratic decision making operates in different ways across different forms of anarchist organisation, with some even rejecting the term 'democracy' (Gordon, 2016), consensus decision making is an important example of how democracy is realised in anarchist and related radical political traditions and is one of the ways we can start to think through how this balancing or negotiation between unrestrained freedom and collectivism might operate in practice and how both *Functional* and *Collective Autonomy* can be realised in anarchist organisation.

Consensus decision making (CDM for short), is described by the Seeds for Change collective as follows:

> Consensus decision making is a creative and dynamic way of reaching agreement between all members of a group. Instead of simply voting for an item and having the majority of the group getting their way, a group using consensus is committed to finding solutions that everyone actively supports, or at least can live with. (Seeds for Change, 2013)

CDM has a rich history both in social movements and in communities such as the First Nations Haudenosaunee Confederation in what we today call North America. It was introduced into left-wing social movements by Quakers who had practised processes similar to CDM for hundreds of years. While I will not explore them in detail here, there are similarities between processes of CDM and the Team Syntegrity or Syntegration protocols developed by Beer and others that were discussed briefly in Chapter 3, and that can also form the basis for reaching consensus in organisations.

In Occupy, CDM was used in various ways in different camps across the movement. While CDM is based on a commitment to reaching consensus, the model is often modified for situations where full consensus is genuinely impossible to achieve, at least within the timeframe available to those involved. In Occupy Wall Street, for example, the practical limitations on achieving consensus in that specific situation – large general assemblies, often including hundreds of participants with varying experiences of and commitments to CDM, at times with urgent decisions to be made – led to CDM being modified. This modified CDM involved introducing forms of majority voting where consensus was unlikely. The threshold required to make a decision here, however, was as high as 90% (Graeber, 2013: 216). For the Occupy activists, this was a way of allowing for effective decision making when consensus would not be possible, but doing so in a manner that avoided the danger of mainstream simple majority decision making, where a decision can leave just shy of half of those involved dissatisfied. Such modified consensus requirements meant that decision making would not grind to a halt but also that the possibility of significantly large minorities being ignored was limited. Importantly, modified CDM is, in many cases, only resorted to after repeated failed attempts at reaching consensus. Consensus is still considered as the primary aim, but modified CDM is put in place as a backup should full consensus prove impossible. Modifying CDM in this way is not the only mechanism that has been put in place to mitigate some of the potential problems associated with it. The practice of 'standing aside' is similarly geared towards allowing for effective decision making while ensuring that minorities are not subjugated to the will of the majority. 'Blocking', by contrast, is a practice that, while also designed to protect minorities, has the potential to completely derail decision making.

In discussing these features of CDM, I am less interested here in the specifics of how CDM is practised and modified and more in the way in which, as anarchist studies scholar Matthew Wilson puts it, 'the *process* used by practitioners can be disentangled from the need to in fact reach consensus' (2014: 151; emphasis in original). In other words, I am more concerned in this discussion with how CDM helps manage collective autonomy than in how or whether consensus – or something close to it – is actually achieved.

Crucially, CDM has the potential to correct for individualist or egoist influences in decision making. Given the aim of CDM of attempting to reach consensus, when compared to forms of decision making based on majorities measured through voting, CDM serves to shift the focus from competition to cooperation and common agreement. How most of us tend to experience democratic decision making, in the parts of our lives where we have any semblance of democracy, is that it involves a contest were two or more positions, perhaps through the provision of arguments and evidence, perhaps through the use of rhetoric or charisma, vie for support. Sometimes, such as in the case of referenda, this amounts to a winner takes all approach, where the size of the minority has no bearing on the decision taken. For example, in the UK's referendum on membership of the European Union in 2016, the 'leave' side won with just under 52% of the vote. In such an example, decision making based on a simple majority – 50% plus 1 vote – results in the choice of a potentially sizeable minority being set aside. Irrespective of what this means for effective decision making, it reflects a competitive version of politics where the aim is to defeat the opponent, something linked both to the kind of liberal and neoliberal individualism previously discussed in this chapter and to a particularly macho approach to debate and decision making (Jaggar, 1985). Whatever form CDM takes, a key part of the process is that individuals are encouraged to share ideas, experiences and opinions in an open and accessible discussion that then aims to find a position everyone can agree on. While this could, of course, be corrupted by particularly manipulative or persuasive individuals, it is at least predicated on an attempt at replacing competition and a drive to win with finding common ground and reflecting the needs and desires of everyone involved. CDM can, therefore, be seen as a way of moving away from a competitive individualism and towards forms of decision making that are more in line with a collectivist approach to autonomy (Kokkinidis, 2014).

As well as the recourse to high-threshold majorities, there are two other common features of CDM worth discussing, each of which potentially make this process more problematic: blocking and standing aside. The practice of blocking or vetoing, common to many forms of CDM, threatens to reintroduce the individualist competitiveness that CDM is, in other respects, well positioned to reject. Blocking, where a single individual involved in a CDM process has the ability to stop a decision being made because of their fundamental opposition to it, is described by Wilson as 'the ability for one individual, or a small minority, to block a decision [and] can lead to a situation where some members of a community are forced to accept the opinions of others' (2014: 152). In other words, by stopping a decision from being made, blocking allows for a group to be dominated by an individual, in so far as that group is prevented from pursuing a course of action that is otherwise desired. While designed to prevent the domination of a small minority by a large majority, blocking also paves the way for the smallest of minorities to dominate the majority. In effect, it creates a back door for the kind of liberal individualist or egoist impact on decision making that the process of CDM mitigates. This is not to say that blocking should have no place in CDM. Indeed, blocking is often used in groups not as a way to prevent a decision being made per se, but rather to indicate the need for further discussion, with a view to consensus hopefully being reached at a later stage. In Occupy Wall Street, for example, when blocking occurred, the individuals responsible for such blocks were invited to share their reasons for doing so, with subsequent attempts often being made to modify proposals in such a way that the block would be withdrawn.

Standing aside, while intended as a way of allowing for decisions to be made in spite of the opposition of small minorities, is still problematic, if considered in relation to the idea of collective autonomy. Standing aside is a practice whereby an individual or a group of individuals may oppose a decision that a large majority is in favour of, but instead of blocking the decision, they indicate that they are happy to see the decision be made so long as they are not party to whatever it entails. In effect, they stand aside from any practical implications the decision may have, while also clearly registering their objection to it. This may have benefits, for instance, in situations where physical confrontation is considered by a large majority to be required in a particular action – such as defending someone from eviction from their home – but where some involved are opposed to any and all forms of violence, even in self-defence. Those opposed may not want to prevent the group from taking that course of action, but do not want to be involved in doing so themselves, as this would compromise their own ethical beliefs. Separate from considerations of whether this is politically or morally valid, I want to address how this relates to the idea of collective autonomy.

Standing aside assumes either a space of autonomy outside the collective in question, as noted by Wilson (2014), or that the autonomy of the individuals involved in standing aside is prior to the collective autonomy afforded by the group. The latter of these assumptions again serves to reintroduce the notion of liberal, individualistic autonomy that CDM provides an alternative to. For this reason, then, it is worth carefully considering whether standing aside can play a role in effective decision making if part of the aim is to root that decision making in a political concept of collective autonomy. Standing aside, furthermore, when understood in this way, comes into conflict with the functional account of autonomy necessary in an anarchist cybernetics, as the individual operating parts of the organisation would have a level of autonomy that existed irrespective of the demands of the organisation as a whole, thus putting at risk the ability of the organisation to respond to complexity and achieve its goals. That standing aside assumes a space of autonomy outside the collective in question is also a problem when viewed in relation to collective and functional definitions of autonomy, but for different reasons. The assumption being made is that there is a pre-existing space of autonomy outside the collective organisational setting that the individual or small group can step aside into. While this may be unproblematic in many situations, where someone can simply stay at home or remain on the side-lines, thinking about anarchist organisation in terms of providing insights into how society as a whole can be organised, it does present a challenge. If autonomy is dependent on collective existing with others, this suggests that there is no space outside that set of collective relationships in which an individual can exist autonomously.

Exclusion

Each of the central definitions of autonomy discussed in this chapter concerns the ways in which autonomy is shaped and constrained by collective, organisational development. The crucial aspect of these definitions that I want to turn to in the remainder of this chapter is what can be considered as the ultimate constraint on autonomy, that of exclusion from the collective entity of the organisation.

For Beer's organisational cybernetics, there must always remain the possibility that any part of the system may be removed from the system if its operation inhibits the system from achieving its goals. If we think about some of the early examples with which cybernetics dealt, such as robotics or mechanical systems, this is quite uncontroversial, but looking at the type of organisation Beer was interested in it raises the prospect of people being made redundant from the firms that were shaped by Beer's consultations. If a department of such a firm is no longer considered functionally effective in the organisation then it can be shut down, and the workers employed there made redundant if they cannot be redeployed elsewhere in the firm. Beer was working as a consultant and writing his early work on cybernetics at a time of near full employment in the UK where, so the anecdote goes, someone could walk out of one job in the morning and be in another by the afternoon. This, of course, is an exaggeration, but it may help explain why, for someone like Beer who by all accounts was relatively progressive in his politics, the thought of making people redundant as a normal part of how an organisation would function could be presented with few ethical quibbles.

For anarchism, this concept of potential exclusion is, in certain ways, far more problematic. On the one hand, many anarchists would reject the link between work – as the means of subsistence – and organisational necessity. A central pillar of most variants of anarchism is the anti-capitalist ideal that no individual will be denied that which they need to survive and to live a full life. Many anarchist approaches to economics are founded on a commitment that society should provide people with all that they need, taking only what people are able to give, encapsulated in the slogan 'from each according to their ability, to each according to their need'. More important for the present discussion, however, is the more general idea of excluding an individual or a group from a collective entity because they no longer contribute effectively to that entity achieving its goals or actually prevent it from doing so. While the tension that exists between *Functional Autonomy* and how anarchists approach the issue of constraint with respect to their conceptions of autonomy is resolvable, through an appreciation of the concept of *Collective Autonomy* (as explained earlier in his chapter), this further tension, over the possible exclusion of individuals or groups from the collective, is potentially more problematic for the ability of anarchist cybernetics to operate as a framework for effective anarchist organisation. Many strands of anarchism are built around communities being radically inclusive of difference, and to raise the prospect of exclusion on the grounds of effectiveness does stand at odds with how anarchism is often conceptualised and practised. That being said, there are many exclusions – for instance, of individuals who routinely engage in sexist or racist behaviour or who because of their actions are seen to have caused or be likely to cause harm to a community – that are part and parcel of anarchist organisation. In the spirit of prefigurative politics, the task may well be to experiment with and negotiate boundaries between exclusion and inclusion rather than to reject exclusion at all costs.

Conclusion

To summarise briefly, in anarchist cybernetics, there are two definitions of autonomy, each referring to different aspects of effective self-organisation. Beer, in his work on viable systems and organisation, introduces the idea of effective freedom, what I have here characterised as *Functional Autonomy*. This is distinct from how we might commonly understand freedom or autonomy, and refers to the scope each of the individual operating units in a system have to take action in their own niches. While such autonomy is required for the organisation to respond to complexity, this autonomy will always be restricted by the need for the organisation to operate as a coherent whole with shared goals. Within anarchism, while there are tendencies towards a liberal or individualist account of autonomy, there is also a clearly articulated understanding of autonomy that mirrors these restrictions as they are articulated in cybernetics. In anarchism, instead of such restrictions coming into play as a result of functional necessity, they play a role in so far as autonomy is conceived of as something constructed by collective organisation. *Collective Autonomy*, as I have termed it here, acknowledges the fact that the freedom individuals have does not pre-exist organisation but is a product of it. As such, individual autonomy is both produced by and restricted by the collective will of the particular organisation or community a person is a member of. Crucially, anarchism suggests how such a process of restricting autonomy can be managed in participatory and democratic ways. Together, *Functional Autonomy*, on the one hand, and *Collective Autonomy*, on the other, are central to a conception of anarchist cybernetics that possesses the ability to inform complex organisational frameworks that are attentive to issues of autonomy and freedom. 'The freedom we embrace', Beer writes, 'must yet be "in control". That means that people must endorse the regulatory model at the heart of the viable system in which they partake' (1974: 88).

6

Communication
(Part I): Information and Noise
in the Age of Social Media

The discussion, thus far in the book, has focused on the functions of self-organisation in anarchist cybernetics. These discussions cover one major aspect of how control is understood in cybernetics (and the anarchist cybernetics I outline in this book), not as domination but as a way of understanding how self-organisation facilitates effective responses to complexity. In Norbert Wiener's original framing of cybernetics, control was one side of understanding how self-organisation operates. The other side was communication. Beer put it similarly when he wrote (1974: 26) that there are three basic tools for coping with complexity and variety: 'the computer, teleprocessing, and the techniques of the science of effective organization'. It is to the former of these, covered under Wiener's use of 'communication', that I turn to in both this and the following chapter.

Earlier, I characterised the nature of communication in the kind of networks that are central to anarchist forms of organisation as many-to-many communication. This refers to the type of networks in which anyone can share information with anyone else. Instead of communication being about two actors speaking to each other in relative isolation (one-to-one communication) or a single actor or small select group broadcasting a message to a larger audience (one-to-many communication), the communication processes of interest in this discussion of anarchist cybernetics are ones that maintain a level of horizontality and equality in terms of opening up both opportunities to speak and to be listened to (many-to-many communication). Understanding communication in this way, as a web or network with limited structural hierarchies, is something that is closely linked to cybernetics. It is an idea that, as I discussed in Chapter 2, does not *necessitate* the kind of radial, anarchist organisation this book is concerned with, but that has nonetheless become intimately connected to how communication is understood in such organisational contexts, largely as a result of the potential it has for minimising structural hierarchy. As that earlier discussion illustrated, the concept of many-to-many, networked communication has also shaped how we understand the ways in which social media platforms might be able to assist anarchist organising. In this chapter, I will return to the discussion of the nature of communication and how this relates to (anarchist) cybernetics, before exploring in more detail what this account of communication means in the age of social media, focusing on the concept of noise and its implications for many-to-many communication.

Cybernetics, information theory and communication

To start with, let's take a look at how communication is understood in cybernetics. In his book *Cybernetics and Management*, Beer describes a system in terms that will be familiar to those acquainted with the basic idea of a communication network. Asking us to imagine a system as a series of dots on a page, Beer writes:

> The connectiveness of the system can now be introduced into this picture by drawing lines between the dots [...] In this way, we come to look upon a system as a kind of network. [...] [t]he lines depicting the network of our system are in fact its *communications*. (Beer, 1967: 10–11, emphasis in original)

In the Viable System Model, introduced in Chapter 3, lines of communication were again identified as being equally important for effective organisation as the different parts of the system are. Indeed, for cybernetics, the organisation of a system is considered to be, in many ways, identical to its communication network. Ashby, for instance, wrote that it is 'quite plausible that we should describe parts as "organized" when "communication" (in some generalized sense) occurs between them' (1962: 257). Prior to the articulation of relationships of collective and functional autonomy and of tactics and strategy, as were discussed in the previous chapters, the parts of any organisation must be in communication. For cybernetic theories of control in systems, one of the key ways in which communication functions is articulated through the concept of 'feedback'.

Feedback is of course now terminology that is commonly used in everyday life, most often in the sense of giving someone feedback, providing them with information that might help them change something like how they perform a certain task. This notion of feedback, as an opinion or report that we can present to someone and that they can use in one way or another, is a slight corruption of how the concept was initially developed. In cybernetics, feedback refers not to a piece of information transmitted between two actors but to a causal loop that helps regulate behaviour in a system. Beer emphasised feedback as 'the most important concept of all' when it comes to understanding self-organisation and control in systems and organisations ([1981] 1994: 32). Feedback can be understood as operating in two ways, positively or negatively, both of which need to be divorced from any normative connotations. Positive feedback refers to a causal relationship where a certain behaviour in one part of a system triggers a response in another part of the system, that then communicates back to the initial part in such a way as to encourage more of the initial behaviour. Negative feedback, in contrast, occurs when the initial behaviour triggers a response such that the information communicated back leads to a decrease in that initial type of behaviour. In the context of thinking about self-organisation and control, feedback is the mechanism whereby a system is able to regulate itself so that any increases in destabilising behaviour or decreases in stabilising behaviour, where one part begins to act outwith the level of functional autonomy allowed of it, are identified and the part responsible for such behaviour is communicated to by the rest of the system so that it reduces or increases that behaviour, allowing the system to maintain equilibrium.

Roel van Duyn, an anarchist and counterculture activist involved in the Dutch Provo movement in the early 1960s and who was influenced by cybernetics, describes negative feedback through considering the of riding a bicycle:

> Take for instance a cyclist. He [sic] follows a particular route
> that he has chosen, and in so doing makes use of a vehicle
> the control of which is essential in this context. How does
> he succeed despite all sorts of disruptive influences from
> outside – such as traffic, conflicting bodily impulses, wind
> and so on – in actually following his route? By steering, by
> exercising constant control. When a gust of wind comes

from the left, he notices a deviation of the cycle to the right
and he turns the handlebars to the left so as to correct the
deviation. If the disturbing influence comes from the right,
with a consequent deviation to the left, then in order to
maintain his direction he turns the handlebars to the right.
(Van Duyn, 1972: 85–6)

Here, the wind that pushes the cyclist to the right or the left causes
a feedback loop whereby the cyclist reacts in such a way that the
behaviour – deviating from the course one way or the other – is
responded to and corrected. The deviation triggers a response that
reduces the deviation. This is how negative feedback operates and, as
Van Duyn explains, self-organisation facilitates control and equilibrium
in a system. Information is communicated through the system – in
this case in the form of a recognition that the course has been diverted
from – that tells part of the system to respond in a particular way – the
handlebars are turned right or left.

While communication between people in an organisation will,
inevitably, involve a whole range of factors, when focusing on
communication in the contexts of a discussion of cybernetics, self-
organisation and control, it is not the content of communication that
is important but the technical, functional role it plays. For cybernetics,
feedback is the concept through which this role is manifest. Thinking
about communication in this way, as a function of viable organisation,
the question is raised as to how communication can best operate
in an effective way to facilitate the kind of self-organised control
that cybernetics and anarchist cybernetics are interested in. While
cyberneticians from Wiener onwards have grappled with this issue,
one of the disciplines that emerged out of and developed alongside
cybernetics was information theory and this field specifically focused
on the question of effective communication in a system. Pioneered by
Claude Shannon and Warren Weaver, information theory articulated a
technical, mathematical approach to communication. I can offer only
the briefest of overviews of the technical aspects of information theory
here, but what information theory can tell us about the problems
effective communication faces is highly relevant for how anarchist
cybernetics might be able to provide a coherent understanding of
communication in anarchist organisation.

Theorising noise in communication

Claude Shannon and Warren Weaver introduced a specific model of communication that aimed to show how signals operated in mechanical and electrical systems. Shannon had been a student of Norbert Wiener's at MIT and was a guest at the Macy Conferences in the 1940s and 1950s, during which cybernetics was shaped as a scientific discipline. As Ronald Kline puts it in his book *The Cybernetics Moment*, Shannon and Weaver aimed to identify 'what was communicated in the messages flowing through feedback control loops that enabled all organisms, living and nonliving, to adapt to their environments' (2015: 12–13). Providing a complete account of communication and, importantly, of the information contained in communication, was central, then, to the primary aim of cybernetics and of their information theory. While cybernetics is concerned with systems in general, for Shannon and Weaver it was electrical systems that were their primary focus and how they understood information reflects this. Kline notes that information, in this context, had a very specific meaning. It was defined as 'the amount of uncertainty involved in the selection of messages by the information source, not as the amount of data selected to be transmitted' (2015: 16). This is a definition that may seem incongruous with how we commonly understand the term, as referring to the content of communication – for instance, the information we pass to one another when speaking – or to that content as manifest in data – for instance, the information we store on computer hard drives.

From the perspective of electrical engineering, information, understood as uncertainty, is important for designing systems. If an engineer is tasked with constructing channels for carrying signals in a system, the potential uncertainty or randomness in the signal transmitted through those channels will determine the capacity required by them. If a transmitted signal has low information – it is highly certain what the message will be, for example a binary of either 1 or 0 – then the channel can be designed to carry such a load. If, however, a transmitted signal has high information – it is highly uncertain what the message will be, for example an analogue signal that could be represented by any fraction between 1 and 0 – then the channel can be designed with a higher capacity for this potential load. This is undoubtedly important when constructing electrical or other technical systems, but how does it relate to what we commonly understand as information and what we think of as communication in an organisation, that is, people speaking to one another and there being meaningful content to their speech? Shannon and Weaver, in their mathematical model of communication

(1949), were not interested in this understanding of information, but this does not mean that information as content or as data cannot be the subject of the analysis they developed. Indeed, as Kline notes (2015), over time there emerged a close relationship between the two definitions of information – as signal uncertainty and as meaningful or semantic content – and the idea of 'the information age' has its roots in both Shannon and Weaver's work and in Wiener's cybernetics.

One of the ways that information theory can be applied to more colloquial understandings of information and communication is through the concept of noise. In a system or organisation, noise refers to the disruption a signal experiences. Given that organisation requires effective communication, a core element of information theory deals with how to counter the presence of noise in a signal. The Shannon-Weaver model of communication, that encapsulates the concerns of information theory, highlights two kinds of noise (Weaver, [1949] 1973: 36). First, 'engineering noise', which refers to 'statistical and unpredictable perturbations' (Shannon, 1949: 11) that impact on the technical account of information. Second, 'semantic noise', which refers to distortions of meaning or to any disruption that inhibits the meaning of a message being received clearly. Effort must be applied, therefore, to remove noise in communication so that it can operate effectively and messages can be clearly transmitted. This is where the common understanding of noise comes in. Anything that disrupts a message, be it the static on a television or radio or even the discomfort caused by sitting in an uncomfortable chair during a lecture, can be considered as noise that is added to the message and that should thus be removed so that the message can come through loud and clear (Fiske, 2011).

As I have highlighted in previous sections of this book, when discussing communication in relation to contemporary anarchist and radical left ideas of organisation what is of primary concern is digital platforms that facilitate many-to-many communication. In other words, social media platforms. In the next chapter I will discuss these platforms in more detail, but for the remainder of this chapter I want to focus on how noise operates in this context. As mentioned earlier, for anarchist cybernetics, a networked or many-to-many account of communication, where everyone can communicate with everyone else in a system, is most appropriate. On social media platforms, for instance, mainstream corporate ones such as Twitter or Facebook, the form of communication at play outside direct messaging functions is not that of one user transmitting information to another user. Instead, users transmit information in the form of tweets or posts, to a large audience of users – either the entire audience of everyone registered or a subset of friends or followers. The information of one tweet or post then becomes part of a stream of similar content that a user scrolls through. Even when algorithms select what users see as they scroll, users are still presented with an information soup from which to select what they want to actually spend time reading and perhaps responding to. Timelines or feeds are, therefore, large collections of potential signals that a particular user chooses to skim over and ignore or focus on and engage with. Only when a tweet or post is actually read, watched or listened to (in other words, received) does it become a signal between users that communicates information.

So what does this mean for an understanding of the role of noise? There may be a temptation to presume that, in this kind of system, barring a poor wifi or mobile data connection, there is no noise. Once we, as users, have selected a tweet or a post to receive, the signal is perfect; we see exactly what the sender transmitted without any interference. While, this is true, it does not remove noise from the equation. For Shannon and Weaver, noise was understood from the perspective of the engineer, designing the system with a view from outside. Human communication can be understood from a similar standpoint, from an outside, third-person perspective. For the most part, however, it is something we experience and something we engage in from a position *within* the communication process. As receivers of messages, then, noise is something we experience as a disruption that makes it difficult for us to understand content. On social media, as individual users faced with streams of potential messages that we scroll through, we are again presented with a distortion that we need to sort through in order to identify messages we really want to receive and spend time on. As we scroll through our timelines, we are engaging in something similar to deciphering a signal in order to determine meaningful content. The difference is that rather than this noise being a property of a unitary signal, it is instead a property of the communication process as a whole. In effect, we experience on social media a mass of noise that must we must wade through in order to find the messages (tweets, posts and so on) that we really want to engage with. The rest, in so far as they are discarded by us, do not qualify as information-rich messages.

Thinking critically about noise

In the next chapter, I will return to this characterisation of social media as transmitting noise to explore how such communication systems themselves, through algorithmic control, attempt to remove this noise in providing information, and the attendant potential through this process for the introduction of hierarchical domination into networked forms of organisation. For now, however, I want to continue this discussion of noise and its potential relevance to anarchist cybernetics by examining how we can think about the presence of noise and the need to correct for it. The picture presented of noise so far here, as a disruption to a signal behind which the true meaning of the message lies, is not one that has gone without critique. There are two broad strands to such critiques: that such a conception of noise fails to recognise that human communication is an interactive process, in which the transmitter and the receiver negotiate meaning; and that, in this conception of noise, communication is reduced to something that is only concerned with functional effectiveness. Both of these lines of critique are important for the discussion of noise and communication in relation to anarchist cybernetics.

Literary critic Roland Barthes's ideas around interaction and the co-production of meaning between authors and readers have been applied to critical accounts of the Shannon-Weaver model of communication (for instance, Díaz Nafría and Al Hadithi, 2009; Resnyansky, 2014). The understanding of communication in information theory, it is argued, is a linear one in which communication involves a direct transmission of information from a source to a receiver. Human communication, however, is seen to be a far more negotiated affair, with the meaning of a message being constructed by both the sender and the person receiving the message. Rather than the meaningful content of a message being precisely what the sender intended, it is something that involves the receiver as much as it does the sender; it is co-constructed or negotiated between them. This is the case even when the message is as clear as a written text that is perfectly reproduced when the message is received, for instance, when the social media post we receive and read is identical in every way to what was typed by the sender. Dealing with noise in communication, therefore, is not as simple as removing disturbance and identifying the 'correct' meaning beneath. A similar critique has been applied to Beer's cybernetics by Werner Ulrich (1981), who argued, in an important and insightful analysis of Project Cybersyn in Chile, that for cybernetics to form a part of participatory forms of organisation, individual actors in communication networks must be able to determine for themselves the meaning in the messages they receive. Indeed, a core aspect of Beer's Viable System Model is that the parts of an organisation are able to determine within their own niches what is required of them, what was defined in the previous chapter as *Functional Autonomy*.

A system of communication that is based on the Shannon-Weaver model entails that the meaning of a message is determined by the sender.

The job of the receiver is merely to take custody of that meaning and, in an organisational setting, apply it. The removal of noise is simply a step in this direct transmission process. In his book *Platform for Change*, written a few years after Project Cybersyn ended, Beer identified 'intelligent' computing as the mechanism by which meaning is determined and noise is corrected for: '[t]he idea is to create a capability in the computer to recognise what is *important*' ([1975] 1994: 431, emphasis in original). As Ulrich comments, '[a]s an action system Cyberstride [the Project Cybersyn computer programme] can impose its autonomy on the allegedly autonomous decision makers' (1981: 52). This calls into question the fundamental character of communication in information theory, but it does not suggest that the removal of noise is something to be rejected entirely. Rather than noise being understood as something that can and should be extracted from a message to reveal the real meaning of the message, noise is instead considered as something that must be grappled with, almost as a third party to negotiations concerning meaning in any act of communication. The process of negotiation will involve sender and receiver not only constructing the meaning of the message but also navigating the presence of noise. As I will show below, this does not mean working towards the removal of noise in its entirety. It instead involves asking questions about which form of noise is most conducive to the kind of communication and organisation that is important in anarchist cybernetics. The challenge, therefore, is to determine how communication networks can best function to allow for negotiation and autonomy, in part through both correcting for certain types of noise by means of their removal and appreciating the important role of other types of noise in constructing meaning.

A further critique of the nature of communication in the Shannon-Weaver model focuses on the treatment of noise in relation to performance and efficiency. Mark Nunes argues that the approach to communication taken by Shannon and Weaver, and by association cyberneticians such as Beer, reflects 'a culture increasingly dominated by a logic of maximum performance' (2010: 4). Communication in these contexts is characterised as part of a command and control process, with noise understood, in Nunes words, as an error: '[e]rror, in effect, communicates information *without a purpose* – or at *cross purposes* to programmatic control' (2010: 12–13, emphasis in original). Control, importantly, is here understood not in terms of self-organisation, as it is elsewhere in this book, but akin to domination. Nunes draws on the work of novelist Umberto Eco and of philosophers Gilles Deleuze and Felix Guattari in identifying in noise a site of potential resistance to this command and control dynamic. Ulrich similarly highlights the potential for noise to provide a site of resistance, in the critique he makes of Project Cybersyn, contending that the aim of Cybersyn was to maximise productivity and, as such, it framed communication as a process of transmission, in which clear orders were to be received by the different parts of the system. 'Cybersyn's built-in purpose', he writes, 'thus appears to be a one-sided *efficiency of production*' (1981: 54, emphasis in original). Or, as Nunes puts it when writing about this form of control more generally, ' "communication" [is reduced] to a binary act of signal detection [that] demands a rationalization of all singularities of expression within a totalizing system' (2010: 5).

Control, understood in this context as domination, what Ulrich calls 'managerial fascism' (1981: 55), is facilitated by a particular form of communication. Insofar as noise is viewed as something that disrupts this form of communication, it has the potential to play a role in resisting such domination. Not only does noise make domination less effective but, as I will turn to shortly, its positioning in the relationship between sender and receiver is not determined by the sender and so it can be utilised, by the receiver, to craft a different meaning to that intended by the sender. As with the critique above, what this suggests is the possibility of taking a position whereby noise is seen as actually productive of autonomy, of the ability of parts of a system or organisation, of actors in a communication network, to determine meaning in a negotiated process between sender and receiver. The issue then shifts from one that is concerned with reducing and even eliminating noise to one that involves autonomous agents shaping the communication process, noise included, in ways that are productive for them.

Gordon Pask's conversation theory

Before turning to one way in which we can think of noise as productive of self-organisation, it should be noted that the characterisation of cybernetics as a field that reduces communication to a linear transmission of meaning from one actor to another is somewhat unfair. While this perspective is undoubtedly present in parts of Beer's work, it is far from a necessary element of cybernetics in general. Gordon Pask, a contemporary of Beer's and one of the key theorists of cybernetics, whose concepts of functional and anatomical hierarchy were discussed in Chapter 3, focuses, in his discussion of self-organisation, on the idea of conversation. Far from defining conversation as a simple transfer of information, for Pask, conversation is a process in which meaning is determined by both parties. Pask's work on conversation (for example, Pask, 1976) is wide-reaching, but fundamentally his argument proposes that it is not simply communication which is synonymous with organisation, but communication understood as conversation. It is through interactions between actors in which agreement is reached that systems become organised. Paul Pangaro, a student of Pask's, summarises conversation theory as follows:

> It is in language, and via conversation, that we live together. In that living, and through agreement, we share perspectives and merge into fractal communities of relations, friends, clubs, schools of thought and entire cultures. Insofar as we share our similarities and (for a moment) ignore our differences, we merge with other participants in conversation and lose our individuality in exchange for 'becoming one with others', at least in the cognitive domain. (Pangaro, 1996)

Relevant to the discussion here concerning social media and how digital platforms can play a role in facilitating communication and self-organisation, Pask worked throughout his life on developing various physical infrastructures that allow such conversations to take place in ways that generate new meanings and agreements. Early in his career, for instance, Pask developed a machine he called Musicolour, that took a musical input and used it to activate a series of light banks. Changes in the music would result in changes in the colours of the lights being activated. Rather than this being a simple matter of certain musical frequencies corresponding directly to specific colours of light, the relationship would change over time so that the musician would need to respond to the coloured lights, and vice versa, in an ongoing, iterative and interactive process. The musician, therefore, was in a form of conversation with the machine whereby their musical performance interacted with the light display. As Andrew Pickering writes, '[e]ventually some sort of dynamic equilibrium might be reached in which the shifting patterns of the musical performance and the changing parameters of the machine combined to achieve synthetic effects' (2010: 316–17). Through this conversation, a state of equilibrium, a form of agreement between performer and machine, is reached. Pask found other ways of manifesting his understanding of conversation and meaning, such as through a form of theatre he created in which audiences could, at key points, select paths for the performance to take, producing a kind of collective 'chose your own adventure' narrative. Here, it is the narrative of the play that is co-created by audience and performers. Pask also worked on an architectural concept, called the Fun Palace, in which a physical environment could adapt to its inhabitants and change over time. Again, the resultant structure is the product of interactive conversation between the physical infrastructure and its inhabitants.

So while there are indeed inclinations, at times even explicit statements, that suggest cybernetics adheres to a model of communication that reduces an interactive process to one of simple transmission, Pask's work shows that an interactive, conversational approach to communication and the co-creating of sensible, meaningful content is consistent with a cybernetic position on self-organisation. Indeed, the importance of an 'ontology of becoming', as Pickering puts it, to second-order cybernetics (discussed in Chapter 3) is relevant here.

Pink noise

Let's return to the discussion of noise, and to how certain forms of noise might be productive in the kind of conversational communication process described by Pask. Although I have often focused on the Occupy movement, and in particular Occupy Wall Street, in this book, the 15M movement in Spain is equally important for discussions of organisation and communication. Shortly after the 15M protests ended, a group of researchers with backgrounds in a range of academic fields began analysing the experience, focusing on how communication operated on social media and, crucially, viewing the protests as a system. Of the insights they gained, their conclusions on the function of noise in the 15M system are crucial to how we might be able to articulate communication processes in anarchist cybernetics. Those involved in the 15M DatAnalysis group, as it became known, were activists involved in the movement and their core concern was not simply studying the protests, but explaining how the movement operated and how participatory self-organisation can be facilitated in and by communication networks. Using methods developed in neuropsychology, which unfortunately I cannot expand on here, the group of researchers collected and analysed data from Twitter, mapping messages and interactions and exploring the forms of noise present in these communication processes. Indeed, rather than simply identifying the presence of noise or instances where noise was absent, the 15M DatAnalysis group highlighted three different forms that noise can take in such a network: white noise, brown noise and pink noise.

White noise 'describes fully random fluctuations with no correlations in time [...] White noise processes display fast changes in their activity but are unable to maintain structured and coherent patterns' (Aguilera et al., 2013: 2). Brown noise,

> resembles a diffusion process with no correlation between increments, but with strong dependencies between the position of one sample and the next [...] Brown noise processes are able to maintain stable structural patterns, but they are unable to flexibly modify their activity when fast changes are required. (Aguilera et al., 2013: 2)

Pink noise, in contrast, refers to 'processes in which an equilibrium is found between the influence of short, medium and long timescales':

> It finds an equilibrium between disordered states with high informational content (white noise) and states with strong memory but low informational content (brown noise). Pink noise processes display dynamics which can maintain stable patterns of activity while being able to flexibly regulate their level of activity. (Aguilera et al., 2013: 2)

These different forms of noise correlate to different forms of organisation. This correlation is based on the fact that the noise present in communication processes, rather than being something that disrupts them, will in fact be productive of the organisational forms those communication processes facilitate. White noise is characterised as random and quickly changing, and so a process of communication in which white noise is present will be part of an organisational form that is unstable, or its presence will not be related to anything that that could be conceived in terms of being an organisation. Brown noise, where the communication process is subject to noise that is highly regular and fixed in variation, will be found in organisational forms that are rigid and unchanging.

For each of these forms of noise – white noise and brown noise – a comparison can be made to how organisation is understood in cybernetics. As I noted in Chapter 3, for Beer and other cyberneticians, there are different forms of system or organisation and each of them is able to respond to complexity and to change in different ways. For strictly organised, hierarchical organisations, that are often cumbersome and slow to react, complexity will be a threat to how well the organisation can operate. If it is slow to respond to complexity its operations will always be a step behind and change will overwhelm the organisation. On the other hand, situations in which separate units enjoy large amounts of flexibility and autonomy may be said to be no organisation at all; the different units will respond to complexity in their own individual niches, but this will not be coordinated in any way and if there ever was an organisation of which they were parts it will cease to operate as a single organisation with set goals. For Beer's cybernetics, and indeed for anarchist cybernetics as I have tried to show throughout this book, the sweet spot between these two extremes is where we find stable self-organising systems and thus organisations. Organisations that achieve this balance between rigidity and dispersion are able to respond to complexity and change while still achieving overarching goals. If brown noise is specific to communication processes in the first type of system – the rigid, predictable one – and white noise the second – the flexible, unpredictable one – then pink noise is important in relation to the third, to the kind of balanced self-organisation that anarchist cybernetics is centrally concerned with.

As such, pink noise in communication is central to achieving a balance between irregular, unpredictable action and regular, predictable action. A form of organisation in which pink noise characterises the communication processes is one that is both stable and possesses a level of flexibility and autonomy. Indeed, it is just this equilibrium between stability and flexibility that is articulated in the concept of *Functional Autonomy* discussed in the previous chapter. While the distinctions between white, brown and pink noise can be understood in mathematical terms, the really interesting thing about these distinctions for issues concerning organisation is the qualitative difference between both the types of noise and the forms of communication and organisation they are associated with. As the researchers involved in the 15M DatAnalysis group argue, pink noise is 'an indicator of distributed self-organisation in a coherent whole: different parts of the system (with their characteristic frequencies) appear globally coordinated in a reciprocal influencing manner' (Aguilera et al., 2013: 3). For them, the *quantitative* properties of white, brown and pink noise can tell us something about the *qualitative* nature of forms of organisation. Different organisational forms involve different processes of communication with different types of noise present in them.

Importantly, this approach takes a step away from the idea that noise must be removed or corrected for. Instead, noise is viewed as productive of different forms of communication and thus organisation. The closest to the situation where the aim might be to remove noise, is the presence of brown noise in a communication practice. Brown noise is predictable and correlates with rigid organisational structures, of the kind critiqued by Ulrich and others in their commentaries on the Shannon-Weaver model and on Project Cybersyn. Such organisational forms are oriented towards maximising a set of simple behaviours and the type of communication that is desired, is that which is functional for achieving this. The kind of organisational situation that Beer was wary of, as is made clear in his rejection of complete autonomy, is linked to the presence of white noise in communication. Again, noise is present, but in a form that correlates with unpredictable, sporadic behaviour, with organisation and communication that is likely to produce this behaviour (sometimes to the point of collapse of the organisation, at least in practical terms). The situations where pink noise is predominant in communication practices strike a balance between these outcomes, correlating, as the 15M DatAnalysis group argues, with self-organisation and, it could be further suggested, with a realisation of *Functional Autonomy*. Organisations with communication processes in which pink noise is present are ones that meet the functional conditions spelled out by Beer in his Viable System Model. They are flexible enough to respond to complexity and change *and* coherent enough to be able to achieve overarching goals. For anarchist cybernetics, and indeed for the 15M DatAnalysis group, these organisational forms and their related communication practices are likely to be engaged in participatory and democratic self-organisation.

Organising noise and communication

At a fundamental level, then, questions of noise and communication are questions of organisation. For cybernetics, organisation is indeed nothing other than nodes in a network connected through communication. While much of the thrust in cybernetics, when it comes to communication and organisation, focuses on minimising or even removing noise from transmissions of information, the insights of the 15M DatAnalysis research group, and from the various critiques of attempts to correct for noise, suggest that the issue is less one of how to ensure that communication processes involve the minimisation or removal of noise and more one concerning how communication can be organised so that noise is present in a form that is productive of participatory and democratic self-organisation. Pink noise reflects organisational and communication processes that can endure over time, quickly relay information through a network and facilitate the achievement of organisational goals. Importantly, for those involved in the 15M DatAnalysis project, this does not point towards blueprints for or prescriptions of what this type of organisation should look like. They share with anarchists an aversion to such directive planning, instead recommending contextual experimentation with practices of self-organisation and participation (as discussed in Swann and Ghelfi, 2019). As one activist involved puts it, 'it is more efficient to share practices, tools and processes to create what could be called a *network econosystem*' (quoted in Swann and Ghelfi, 2019: 12, emphasis in original). In other words, in a manner akin to the prefigurative approach to politics discussed elsewhere in this book, organisations must develop and test practices in order to identify what allows them to self-organise effectively. The lesson of this discussion of noise, therefore, is that this experimentation should take into account the productive capacity of pink noise and establish what communication processes embody it.

When I discussed the work of Pask earlier in this chapter, I highlighted how he applied his account of communication as conversation to interactions between humans and machines, and between humans and other forms of infrastructure. This is something we need to keep in mind if we want to consider experimentation with the kind of digital social media platforms that might facilitate self-organisation. Like the 15M DatAnalysis activist researchers, Pask insisted that any interaction between humans and machines in communication processes should involve the structures framing these interactions being capable of experimentation and changing over time. This is reflected in his Fun Palace experiment; while this was a physical architectural structure rather than a digital one, the aim was that different configurations could be tried and tested, by means of users adapting the space through their interactions with it. The form of control here was the balancing between flexible autonomy and rigid prescription (as is encapsulated in the concept of *Functional Autonomy*) and the communication process is one co-created by the actors involved (including non-human actors). As Pickering puts it, drawing on Pask's related work on computers, 'the built environment and its inhabitants' use of it co-evolve open-endedly in time in ways neither the architect, nor the computer, [...] could have foreseen' (2010: 377). Turning to digital platforms that facilitate self-organisation, these too must be fundamentally open-ended and adaptable. While a platform like Facebook may have several features that are useful when it comes to anarchist organisation, ultimately it is a closed system that the users have no control over. What a cybernetic approach to communication and self-organisation demands, in contrast, is something more akin to an open source platform, where users can craft the infrastructure as they engage with it and modify it over time. Ultimately, such a platform ought to reflect the underlying values and principles of prefigurative politics that are discussed throughout this book.

This demand for open, experimental platforms is, of course, an incredibly vague requirement that says little about precisely how such a platform would operate. The insights concerning noise in this chapter lead to similarly general conclusions, in terms of requirements for the design of communication processes and infrastructures. While the 15M DatAnalysis research tells us that communication networks that feature pink noise are those that are self-organised in durable and effective ways, this points only to a correlation and not to specific features of communication that produce pink noise and which could then said to be conducive to self-organisation. Through combining the insights of both Pask and the 15M DatAnalysis group, what we can propose is that communication practices should be conversational and interactive, and should be characterised by the presence of pink noise. Beyond this, however, there may be little that can concretely be recommended to those wanting to organise in participatory and democratic ways. Of considerable relevance though, is that the kind of experimentation this approach calls for, the kind of prefigurative action that is central to anarchist cybernetics, has been going on for quite some time. Since at least the 2011 uprisings, activists have grappled with using and adapting social media platforms, both mainstream ones and independent or alternative ones. Prior to that attempts were made to utilise the internet more generally as an important part of infrastructures that would allow for the kind of self-organisation that is so important to both cybernetics and anarchist politics. By examining the results of these experiments, and the attendant frustrations frequently expressed by activists involved in them, perhaps there are useful lessons to be learned about how communication can operate to support self-organisation.

Conclusion

This chapter has attempted to outline both how communication might feature in anarchist cybernetics and how it can be productive of self-organisation. For cyberneticians, like Ashby and Wiener, organisation is nothing other than communication. For Pask, similarly, it is conversation, interactive communication through which meaning is co-created, that provides the foundation on which self-organisation can be built. While there is a tendency in cybernetics, and in the information theory of Shannon and Weaver, towards viewing communication in terms of efficiency and the effective transmission of information, the conversation-focused approach of Pask, particularly as it is articulated by Pickering, ties in far more closely with the ideals of participatory democracy that motivate anarchist cybernetics. On this account, noise, rather than being something to be simply removed from signals, is understood in far more nuanced terms, as something that exists in different forms in communication processes and that is productive of different kinds of organisation. Pink noise, as understood by the activist researchers involved in the 15M DatAnalysis group, encapsulates the conditions required for self-organisation: it is durable over a long time, flexible enough to respond to change and complexity, yet still coherent enough to allow for broad organisational goals to be achieved. Thus, instead of anarchist organisations seeking to remove noise, anarchist cybernetics proposes that pink noise, as an aspect of interactive, conversational communication, actually plays an important role as an indicator of self-organisation. The analysis provided in this chapter suggests some general necessary conditions for self-organisation, at least in terms of the communication processes involved. In the next chapter, I want to take this further and explore how real engagements with digital and social media platforms can begin to help outline some of the core features of the communication practices required by anarchist cybernetics.

7

Communication (Part II): Building Alternative Social Media

Communication is, of course, something we engage in all the time, both within and outwith organisational settings. For Beer, the kind of communication at work in self-organisation and viable systems ranges from informal conversation during tea breaks to that of formal communication systems and dedicated infrastructures. From a cybernetic perspective, communication is something functional to effective organisation. For anarchist cybernetics the same is true. While communication plays many roles in our day-to-day lives, when thinking about self-organisation, it is the functional value of specific forms of communication that are of interest. In Occupy Wall Street, the communication that allowed it to function in participatory and democratic ways included the highly structured processes of the general assembly and spokes-council, as well as the conversations that camp members were having with one another throughout the days and weeks that the camp was in place. In this chapter, I want to build on the previous discussion to explore how functional communication with respect to self-organisation might be supported by technology. Given the articulation of communication as conversation in Pask's cybernetics, it is social media, that is, communication technologies that privilege interaction over direct broadcasting, that I will discuss here. Rather than examining the potential of existing platforms, such as Facebook, for self-organisation, I want to consider how bespoke, alternative social media might support and reinforce collective self-organising processes. The aim here is to provide an outline of the organisational (rather than technical) functions that such a social media platform might need to include if it is to aid effective self-organisation, doing so by drawing on the discussions of control and communication throughout this book so far.

Alternative media

A useful place to begin thinking about the kind of alternative social media platforms that lend themselves to anarchist and radical organisation is the literature on alternative media in general. At least since the Levellers, the egalitarian populist movement of mid-17th-century England, who pioneered the use of pamphlets as a means of communication, radical political groups have always valued the production of media. This has included printed material such as pamphlets, flyers and newspapers, as well as broadcasted messages through, for example, film or, more recently, the internet. Often, these media have been characterised as 'alternative media'. They are seen as separate from mainstream media, like television networks and large newspaper publishers, and are intended to communicate a group's political message to the public. It is the tension between the nature of this kind of alternative media and that of mainstream media that I want to focus on in this section. Mitzi Waltz describes alternative media as 'media that are alternative to, or in opposition to, something else: mass-media products that are widely available and widely consumed' (2005: 2). Here, the alternative is defined in terms of being against the qualities of something else, something that it opposes and is differentiated from, that it rejects and provides an alternative to. In an almost dialectical move, alternative media is understood as being a negation, in part or in full, of mainstream media. Identifying and critiquing the key characteristics of mainstream media, such as their corporate ownership, funding structure and their position in the matrix of political power, alternative media embody alternatives to such characteristics and attempt to manifest them in different structures.

Specifically, anarchist discussions of alternative media highlight participation as one of the key aspects of such critical alternatives. In contrast to mainstream media's exclusion and gatekeeping, in terms of who actually gets to be part of producing content, an anarchist approach prioritises, in the words of Jeff Shantz, an 'active membership system based on solidarity and mutual aid' (2010: 52). Linking this to a critique of the economics of mainstream media, Shantz goes on to argue (2010: 52) that '[t]his participatory arrangement helps to alleviate tendencies towards a consumerist model that separates producers and users, with distinctions in power and control within the infrastructure.' Sandra Jeppesen and others in the Collectif de

Recherche sur l'Autonomie Collective (Research Group on Collective Autonomy) similarly argue for participatory and democratic media, grounding their case in a prefigurative politics 'where media activists create anti-hierarchical organizations in the here and now' (Jeppesen, et al., 2014: 11). I discussed prefiguration at length in Chapter 4, but to recap quickly, this is the idea that the ends of anarchist politics – freedom, mutual aid and so on – should be reflected or embodied in the means used in the immediate present to try and achieve those ends. For anarchist alternative media, then, the image of what media would look like in an ideal anarchist society ought to inform that which is created today. Indeed, Jeppesen et al. define anarchist or anti-authoritarian media collectives as those that 'establish economic and organizational forms that prefigure cooperative futures and build strong relationships with broader social movements while simultaneously creating counter-hegemonic content and counter-publics around interlocking issues of poverty, race, gender, colonialism and sexuality' (Jeppesen at al., 2014: 3).

Defining alternative media, therefore, involves both a critique of mainstream media and an articulation of an alternative to the mainstream media. The former is vital because part of creating an alternative to something demands an analysis of that thing. Without such an analysis, it would be impossible to work out what is required of the alternative. In this chapter, I want to attempt just such an analysis of mainstream social media and a subsequent envisioning of alternative social media, a vision of the kind of digital communication platforms that might help facilitate self-organisation. Before outlining some of the necessary parameters for and features of alternative or anarchist social media, a critique of mainstream social media needs to be engaged in. There are four related critiques that an anarchist analysis of mainstream social media foregrounds. By mainstream social media, I am here thinking in particular of platforms such as Facebook and Twitter. Essentially, as discussed elsewhere in this book, my interest here is in digital platforms that act as infrastructures for many-to-many communication. Given this definition of social media, how do mainstream platforms shape or regulate this communication in ways that are antithetical to platforms that would encourage participatory and democratic self-organisation?

Four critiques of social media

The first critique of social media, one that perhaps arises most frequently in everyday debate, is centred around privacy and the collection of data from users. One of the defining features of social media platforms is that they harvest data about users' behaviour and relationships. While this feature provides the starting point for the other critiques discussed here, the lack of privacy users enjoy on social media platforms has been raised as an issue in its own right. While the direct threat of surveillance of individuals through social media, by corporations or governments, is important, what is of equal concern is how the collection of users' data – often called 'big data' because of the vast amounts of data that mainstream social media use allows these social media companies to collect – is used by advertisers and political campaigners. The collection of big data facilitates far more than straightforward surveillance. Rather than social media companies acting like a contemporary, tech-savvy equivalent of the Stasi, with a file on every user, big data allows them to map social networks and provide access to specific demographic groups (Fuchs (2014) provides an interesting overview of the debates around privacy and social media). Often, this will simply manifest in the form of targeted advertising, where the behaviour of a user online will produce data that is then utilised to target adverts at that user specifically based on their online behaviour, as well as potentially providing advertisers with knowledge of and access to similar users. If you watch a lot of videos on YouTube on a certain topic, you might start seeing related advertising on other online platforms that you use. Social media apps on your phone can even listen in to what is happening in your immediate environment to identify keywords that are then used to immediately target you with relevant adverts.

Increasingly, however, concern around privacy and the collection of user data has been linked to political campaigning. In 2017 and 2018, it was revealed by whistle-blower Christopher Wylie that data analysis company Cambridge Analytica had gained access to the personal data of millions of Facebook users and used this to target political advertising to key demographics (Cadwalladr, 2017). This involved specific adverts being used to target specific groups in ways that were designed to influence their behaviour. Of course, all political campaigning is geared towards influencing behaviour. A poster put up during an election, for instance, is intended to convince people to vote for this party or that candidate. What Cambridge Analytica was doing, however, was using personal data about groups of social media users to tailor adverts in ways that would appeal directly to them. Rather than everyone seeing the same poster, different people would see different posters aimed at catching their attention and interest, through the adverts' use of specific knowledge about them gleaned from the personal data collected through social media, material that would thus appeal directly to them as individuals. Such targeting online was not solely designed to encourage people to vote for a certain candidate; there is also evidence that it was used to suppress turnout in certain areas. The personal data collected by Facebook in particular, it was suggested, allowed for massive and complex manipulation of voter behaviour and has been linked to the results of the 2016 presidential election in the US and the UK vote to leave the EU in the Brexit referendum of the same year.

Interestingly, Beer warned of something like this use of information technology as early as 1974, when, in *Designing Freedom*, he wrote of computers creating a model of the public through the use of data. He finds it 'alarming that private concerns are able to build systems of this type, without anyone's even knowing about their existence' and comments on 'an evident risk in installing a model of the public in the computer [...] [that] might be misused by a despotic government or unscrupulous management' (1974: 34). And again: 'we allow publishers to file away electronically masses of information about ourselves – who we are, what are our interests – and to tie that in with the mail order schemes, credit systems, and advertising campaigns that line us all up like a row of ducks to be picked off in the interest of conspicuous consumption' (1974: 63).

The second critique of mainstream social media is one that focuses on political economy. The big data that makes the kind of manipulation witnessed in the likes of the Cambridge Analytica scandal possible, is, of course, dependent on mass usership of such platforms. Without users, social media companies have no data, and without huge numbers of users the kind of network and preference mapping that is taking place on a previously unimaginable scale would be unachievable. Importantly, the fact that platforms like Facebook and Twitter are free to use is central to the development of such mass engagement. According to the type of political economic analysis conducted by Marxist theorists, such as Christian Fuchs (2014), this equates to a situation of economic exploitation. In a Marxist understanding of political economy, exploitation refers to the difference between the value produced by labour and the wage provided to the labourer being taken as surplus by the capitalist. In a formal sense, labouring for a wage is exploitative because that labour produces more value than is returned in the form of the wage. This surplus value is taken by the capitalist even though they have not laboured to produce it. On social media platforms, it is argued, similar conditions are created and maintained. Everything we do on social media – posting, liking, sharing, commenting and so on – creates data, access to which is sold to advertisers or political campaigns. The data we produce as users, through activity that can be considered labour, is transformed into value for social media companies. The difference between this form of exploitation and that of waged labour, Fuchs writes, 'is that users are unpaid and therefore infinitely exploited' (2014: 110).

Others have argued, along similar lines, that not only is the labour of social media activity infinitely exploitative but it is also managed in the way other forms of labour are managed in the workplace. As Beverungen et al. put it:

> When Facebook employees code algorithms for data extraction, or develop protocols like the 'Like' button, they are effectively managing. They are guiding user behaviour in such a way that it is more likely to create marketable data, or generate content that will draw other users' attention, which can subsequently be commodified via advertising. (Beverungen et al., 2015: 483)

In recent years, of course, this critique has also been applied to a range of apps and games that are free to download and play. While they might not involve the same level of interaction that social media encourages and thus there is a more limited potential for social network data to be gathered, personal data about individuals is nonetheless captured and packaged as commodities. Approaching the critique of social media with this type of political economic analysis in mind also serves to draw attention to the material aspects of digital media. Fuchs (2014: 119–20) highlights the manual labour that goes into mining the minerals required for producing the physical devices used to access digital media, such as smartphones and tablet computers, as well as the conditions of labour in the factories assembling these devices. The material economic cost to human beings, in places like China and the Democratic Republic of Congo, of making digital media possible ought also to be taken into consideration when discussing the appropriateness of social media platforms for anarchist and radical organising. This is especially true if such organising is framed in terms of prefigurative politics. Can action aimed at bringing relationships of solidarity and mutual aid into being be based on such dire and exploitative working conditions?

The third critique of mainstream social media platforms identifies the potentially problematic nature of the kind of relationships social media produces between users. This critique, as expressed by authors such as Evgeny Morozov (2011) and Jodi Dean (2009), takes a perhaps pessimistic position on the 'weak ties' that are created between social media users. Strong ties, it is argued, are required for stable political organisation, while weak ties are considered to be difficult to translate into offline relations and engagements that demand an obligation on the part of those involved. While social media may be built on interaction and many-to-many communication, as the previous discussions in this book have hopefully made clear, this communication and these connections between nodes in networks are only interesting from the perspective of anarchist cybernetics in so far as they constitute organisation. The weak ties critique suggests that, with respect to mainstream social media, while communication takes place and so some form of system exists, this is not adequate for the creation and development of the form of organisation that Beer's Viable System Model might apply to. It should also be noted, however, that such mainstream networks do produce an outcome that has been called the 'strength of weak ties'. Graham Jones argues that the weak ties of social media platforms and similar networks open up possibilities for forming a greater number of weak ties than are formed through organising that is based purely on strong ties, with the quantity of ties proving more important than their quality (whether they are weak or strong):

> Supposing, for example, you find a person on social media who has a lot of connections, but none or only a few are mutual friends of yours. They are a vital organ in a community which you are cut off from. Extending into their networks, then, will open up a huge swathe of new contacts. A different person may have a far higher number of friends; however, if they are mostly already people you know, connecting with them is unlikely to open up new areas of the network. (Jones, 2018: 60)

The fourth line of critique I want to consider here, one that in a way brings the three previous critiques together, relates to the forms of behaviour and of thinking that social media platforms produce and reinforce. The subjectivity of users – that is, the agency and potential for thought and action individuals have – is, on mainstream social media platforms, conditioned towards individualism. This contrasts with the kind of subjectivity that is desired for anarchist self-organisation, which requires collective subjectivity, of the kind outlined in Chapter 5 as *Collective Autonomy*. Mainstream social media platforms steer users towards an individualistic mindset, whereby they view themselves as entrepreneurial producers of content that they exchange for quantified reward in the form of likes and shares. Social media has been understood as shaping human neurophysiology (Terranova, 2012) in ways that lead to such individualism becoming dominant. Jodi Dean, for instance, writes that online communication 'reformats ever more domains of life in terms of the market: *What can be bought and sold? How can a practice, experience, or feeling be monetized?*' (2009: 32, emphasis in original). The subjectivity critique, then, contends that the way behaviour on social media is shaped, through how the structure of interactions is enabled and restricted, moulds individual users into the kind of individualist agents or subjects that are desired by neoliberal economic theory. By encouraging maximising behaviour in relation to the quantity of likes and shares, for example, the *homo economicus* (economic man [*sic*]) of neoliberal economics is produced.

Linking this to the discussion of individualism in Chapter 5, rather than product of the organisational arrangements of social media being *Collective Autonomy*, as would be desired for anarchist self-organisation, it is an egoistic individualism that emerges. Importantly, as Eva Giraud argues (2015: 130), this turns our private selves and our social relationships into commodities that we then trade on social media; these platforms 'are seen as connecting individual subjects with consumer capitalism, making public our private selves, in order to transform the self into a set of resources'. This critique of mainstream social media platforms brings together the other three critiques discussed in this section, by highlighting how the managing of behaviour in the political economy of social media produces specific forms of relationship that construct specific individualistic subjectivities. This serves, however, to frame the issue of subjectivity as a one-way street, with the users being completely at the mercy of platforms with respect to subjectivity formation and agency. As Giraud and other authors, such as Beverungen et al. (2015), note, social media platforms can also be a site of resistance, through which subjectivities, rather than merely being shaped by the hierarchical structure of the platforms, are contested and produced differently. Such contestation involves users subverting or appropriating the mechanics of the platforms to produce more collectively oriented subjectivities, and as such the kind of subjectivities that are more closely aligned with notions of *Collective Autonomy* and participatory, democratic self-organisation. While this is a vital avenue that needs to be further explored in critical discussions of social media, in the remainder of this chapter, I instead want to focus on how platforms could be redesigned, or designed from scratch, in ways that help facilitate self-organisation and the kind of interactions required by anarchist cybernetics.

Building alternative social media

The cybernetic account of self-organisation, and how this is applied in anarchist cybernetics, is not predicated on the use of digital media or information systems. We live in a world in which digital information is so ubiquitous that even speaking of something like an 'information age' (Kline, 2015) is in many ways gratuitous. As the saying goes, fish don't have a word for water. But against the backdrop of digital mediation, it is easy to forget that in person, face-to-face communication is still the primary way most organisation happens. In spite of activists keenly embracing the internet around the turn of the millennium, the majority of real organising, where decisions are made and action is taken, still primarily takes place through groups meeting in person. It is crucial that this is kept in mind when discussing digital media platforms like social media, especially ones that might begin to mitigate for the kind of problems highlighted by the critiques of social media discussed here. When we explore alternative social media platforms that are designed specifically for self-organisation, we need to remember that these ought to be seen as aids for offline organising, and as such, as infrastructures that support face-to-face discussion and action rather than as an entirely separate sphere that radical politics can inhabit.

Jeff Shantz similarly characterises online media as primarily existing to support broader infrastructures for organisation, quoting one anarchist media activists describing them as 'an aspect of cognition' and 'externalised cognitive facilities' (2010: 52). Alternative social media platforms, then, can be characterised as providing a set of mechanisms that facilitate and reinforce collective self-organisation, an external scaffold for developing *Collective Autonomy*. As with Beer's Viable System Model and the anarchist version of it introduced in Chapter 3, the discussion I want to present here focuses less on the specific form such a platform might take and more on the functions it might include, or rather, the functional elements of self-organisation its features might facilitate. This discussion will, therefore, be necessarily somewhat vague as to specifics, and without a background in the technical design of social media and other applications I am not in a position to offer anything more than a sketch of the functions of a potential alternative system.

One important point to clarify, before beginning, is the precise nature of these alternatives as relates to and is contrasted with that of mainstream platforms. As I noted at the start of this chapter, an alternative is defined as something that picks out key characteristics of something and offers an alternative to them, that reflects an opposition to, rejection and critique of, these characteristics. Decaffeinated coffee, for instance, is an alternative to coffee in so far as it removes the caffeine. Renewable energy is an alternative to fossil fuels in that it does not involve extraction of finite resources. The alternative mirrors the original in some respects but negates one or more aspects of that original. Crucially, however, this is not a pure negation. The entirety of the original is not rejected, only some key features of it. Decaffeinated coffee still tastes more or less like coffee (perhaps depending on who you ask). Renewable energy still provides electricity. Andrew Pickering notes that the idea of an alternative – or as he phrases it an 'anti'-something; decaffeinated coffee as anti-coffee, for example – entails '*another* or *different* approach that crossed the terrain of established forms' (2010: 370, emphasis in original). In discussing alternative social media, then, the purpose is not to propose infrastructures that negate every aspect of mainstream social media, because, inevitably, these would no longer then be social media. A true or complete negation would involve the creation of an anti-social media, removing not only the negative aspects of mainstream social media that the various critiques of such identify but also the many-to-many, interactive nature of the communication that is desired. In so far as this discussion deals with alternatives, this involves maintaining those aspects of mainstream social media that are not objectionable, indeed that are viewed as desirable, such as their practical user interface or their ability to extend social networks. The alternative is, as Pickering says, 'another' or 'different' to the mainstream.

Design

While work on alternative media (for example, Rauch, 2014; Sandoval and Fuchs, 2010) highlights a distinction between the form media take and the content broadcast on them, with respect to alternative social media, a more relevant distinction is between form and design. Discussions of form consider the functional role different platform mechanisms might play in relation to self-organisation. A focus on design, on the other hand, allows us to explore how platforms are developed with a view to facilitating such a form. In the previous chapter, I introduced the idea of the Fun Palace in relation to Pask's cybernetics. Pickering describes the Fun Palace as follows: 'If mainstream architecture aspired to permanent monuments, aesthetic and symbolic forms drenched in meaning, and fitness to some predefined function, the Fun Palace was envisaged as just a big and ephemeral rectangular box from the outside and a 'kit of parts' on the inside' (Pickering, 2010: 370).

The 'kit of parts' on the inside meant that those inhabiting the Fun Palace could shape and reshape their physical environment over time, in response to their own needs and desires. This approach to architecture and design sits well with the prefigurative drive of anarchist cybernetics, with the design process involving experimental trial and error. Ana Paula Baltazar (2007) makes an explicit connection between open processes of architectural design and anarchism, outlining her 'cyberarchitecture' as 'developing tools or interfaces for possible self-organisation from the bottom up' (2007: 1238).

Baltazar applies this approach to the design of digital information systems and shows how this idea, of users having control over the design process of a physical environment, can operate as a framework for the design of digital platforms. Baltazar highlights four aspects of a participatory and democratic design process (2007: 1247–8):

1. the easiness to try things out and undo them;
2. the self-revealing flexibility enabled by the design (interface), because if it is not apparent it will not be used;
3. the easiness to use for first timers, though not banal to experts; and
4. the pleasure and fun in using design (interface), so people will not need to concentrate their efforts in learning the environment but on playing.

The design of alternative social media platforms, therefore, ought to be structured in such a way that non-expert users are able to engage in the design process and through doing so structure the digital environment they inhabit in ways that support their collective self-organisation, in an analogous manner to how the Fun Palace allowed people without any architectural design skills to co-create their physical environment. Crucial to this is a suitably low barrier to entry for design so that those without technical expertise can play a role. If the processes for creating, developing and evolving alternative social media platforms that are to be used to support self-organisation are not themselves subject to participatory and democratic self-organisation, then some of the problems of mainstream social media, in terms of systems managing behaviour, will be replicated. A central focus of anarchist cybernetics, as highlighted throughout this book, is the need for participatory and democratic methods that provide an appropriate structure for shaping the autonomy that it is desired individuals or parts of organisations possess. A participatory design process of the type described by Baltazar provides for this, without reintroducing the kind of domination created by mainstream social media platforms that anarchists are opposed to.

One of the ways of bridging the skills gap between expert and non-expert users of digital platforms when it comes to design is to enable the easy combination of various off-the-shelf applications in a single platform, thus allowing users of that platform to design its environment to meet their needs. While this requires a level of expert knowledge with respect to the development of the individual applications (which could include calendars, direct messaging functions, photo galleries, shared maps and so on), the user-designers combining these applications need only select and insert the desired options into their platforms. In this way, platforms could be customised to specific groups of users without those users having to learn how to build a social media platform from the ground up. Like the Fun Palace's 'kit of parts', a design suite could include a range of applications that users could combine in different ways to create different niche-specific platforms. Werner Ulrich – whose critique of Project Cybersyn was highlighted in the previous chapter – makes the point, in relation to cybernetics and design, that 'all design tools represent *somebody's* solution to *somebody's* problem' (1981: 33, emphasis in original). Through a user-friendly design process that provides various building blocks for effective digital platforms, a participatory design process can be put into practice that represents user's solutions to their own problems. Beer himself puts it well in *Designing Freedom* when he writes:

> For the first time in the history of man [*sic*] science can do whatever can be exactly specified. Then, also, for the first time, we do not have to be scientists to understand what can be done. It follows that we are no longer at the mercy of a technocracy which alone can tell us what to do. Our job is to start specifying. (Beer, 1974: 56)

In other words, a participatory design process will involve non-specialists telling specialists what they need form their technology.

This approach to design identifies technology as a site of social relations (as recognised by Pierre-Joseph Proudhon (Truscello and Gordon, 2013)). The aim, in the context of anarchist cybernetics, therefore, is to ensure that the technology of self-organisation is a site of participatory and democratic social relations and of mutual aid. As

John Clark puts it, anarchist, prefigurative technological development must reflect the following:

> comprehensibility; compatibility with aesthetic values; feasibility of continual reassessment and fundamental redesigning in relation to analysis of needs; multifunctionality; capacity to fulfil basic human needs; [...] incompatibility with technocratic and bureaucratic structures; compatibility with democratic control of society, decentralized decision-making, and non-hierarchical social structures; conduciveness to production process involving enjoyment, creativity, and human development. (Clarke, 1984: 197)

Form

As foregrounded previously, the aim of this discussion is not to provide a fixed blueprint for an alternative social media platform. Rather, the previous section argues that any design process ought to be participatory and democratic, responding to the specific needs of users and being capable of adapting and changing as those needs develop over time. Nonetheless, with some of the broad necessary functions of effective anarchist organisation highlighted throughout this book in mind, it is possible to sketch, in very broad terms, the mechanisms and functionality necessary for this kind of digital platform.

First, what communication functions would an alternative social media platform need to include?

Forums for conversation The requirement for conversational, many-to-many communication, of the type that, for cyberneticians like Beer and Pask, is at the heart of self-organisation, must be facilitated by an alternative platform. Forums, understood broadly to included traditional internet forums, Facebook-style groups and messenger app groups such as those on WhatsApp, could fulfil this core function.

Direct messaging In addition to supporting many-to-many communication, alternative platforms would need to provide the facility for users to send direct messages to one another. One of the strengths of an alternative could be the capacity to provide for all forms of online communication within one platform, and so something equivalent to an email function would also be necessary.

Sharing content with meme/viral potential A key strength of mainstream social media is the ability to 'like' content that a user has posted and to then share that content with other users. Content on social media can then snowball, as it is shared from user to user throughout the network. This is one of the central functions of social media and how it functions to spread information. In so far as alternative social media might replicate some of the desired functions of mainstream news media, this type of functionality would provide an important means of transmitting content that individuals might otherwise never come across.

News feed with curated and user–generated content Newsfeeds or timelines are the key ways in which users view content on social media and would need to be replicated on any alternative platform. How these would be generated, however, would need to come under scrutiny, with the algorithmic control function of mainstream platforms eschewed in favour of functions that would be more open to user control, both in terms of what individual users wanted to view and collectively with respect to protocols for curating content. Beer makes this point when he acknowledges with characteristic prescience that '[t]he editorial decision is the biggest variety attenuator that our culture knows. […] [T]he cybernetic answer is to turn over the editorial function to the individual, which may be done by a combination of computer controlled search procedures of recorded information made accessible by telecommunications' (1974: 62). Relating this to complexity and variety, this process of user-curation or user-generation of information is a central aspect of how variety attenuation and amplification (discussed in Chapter 3), is realised technologically.

Public relations function For activist-type groups, communicating beyond their own networks is vital and as well as an alternative platform allowing users in groups to collaborate in creating such externally focused content, it could also include functions for distributing this content, either to the general audience of all other users or even to specific media outlets (for example, the collaborative element could include an easy way to construct press releases and send these to relevant media contacts).

Linking alternative and mainstream platforms One of the failures of many existing alternative platforms is that they become an added burden, as to users' time and commitment, on top of their engagements with the platforms that they are already using. Mechanisms whereby an alternative platform would allow for content to be cross-posted to different platforms, or through which the feeds and messages from different platforms could be displayed, would minimise some of the barriers to access and increase their reach. Social media management tools already provide some of this functionality.

Central resource hub As well as providing a range of one-to-one and many-to-many communication mechanisms, an alternative social media platform could also house a set of resources for self-organisation, such as information for effective and safe online communication or for offline organising and direct action.

Noise and overload filters Chapter 6 focused on the issue of noise in many-to-many online communication, concluding that, rather than being how to remove noise from messages, the real concern is how to shape communication in such a way that the noise in the system is productive of self-organisation. Mainstream social media platforms rely on algorithmic control to filter for noise and reduce the amount of information users see so that they do not experience overload. On Facebook and Twitter a user never sees everything that their friends or the people they follow post. An alternative platform would need to ensure that filtering for noise and overload was, at the very least, open to democratic oversight, if not the product of direct participatory engagement, for instance through popular content floating to the surface, as it were, through a voting procedure. This functionality is another key part of how a social media platform can help attenuate variety. This is potentially a highly complex affair, however, as the aim is not to eliminate noise but craft it in specific ways. As with other elements of this proposal, however, this would have to be subject to trial and error experimentation, in line with prefigurative design principles.

Overuse addiction warning system While the kind of digital platform I am sketching here is intended to be something useful for self-organisation, it must be recognised that social media use does come with well-documented side-effects for individual users related to addiction and overuse. To ensure effective self-organisation, an alternative platform ought to be able to warn users that they are spending too much time on the platform, perhaps with a forced time-out function. Second, how might an alternative platform best function as a kind of information management system to aid in the processes related to, for example, tactics, strategy and grand strategy, and *Collective Autonomy*, which have been discussed throughout this book?

General assembly function As discussed in Chapter 3, one of the central aspects of the anarchist version of Beer's Viable System Model is the ability for the workings of functional higher levels of the system to be conducted in forums in which everyone involved in that particular organisation can directly participate (or indirectly influence decisions through a delegate system). These previous discussions made comparisons with the general assemblies of the Occupy camps. While online assemblies of this sort, with potentially thousands of participants, have rarely, if ever, been made a reality, as this is a key function of effective self-organisation, an alternative platform could experiment with methods designed to replicate this strategic and grand strategic functional layer of participatory and democratic decision making. Decision-making-oriented video conferencing could provide a potential option in this regard.

Pad function To assist in facilitating online discussion and decision making, collaborative pads could play an important role in an alternative digital platform. Collaborative pads allow for multiple users to view and edit a text document in real time, and have been used as a tool for writing meeting agendas and minutes in a participatory way. Of course, once there are more than a handful of users this can become a very messy affair, but again, this is something worthy of experimenting with, given that a central aim of such collaborative working is to limit the centralisation of organisational power through limiting who is involved in setting agendas and reporting back on discussions.

Memory/narrative Given the importance of strategy and grand strategy in anarchist cybernetics, functionality in an alternative digital platform to support long-term planning, for example through facilitating a narrative- or memory-focused layer to communication and organising, would be essential. This would entail a shift away from the short-term stream-centred approach of mainstream social media, where users experience content as isolated posts with little relation to what has come before them or what will follow them.

File sharing and knowledge exchange Alternative social media platforms would also need to include mechanisms for the exchange of knowledge and information beyond simple messages, for example, through file sharing or document storage functions that make collaborative editing possible. This would mirror the way online co-working platforms operate, by integrating such functionality into interactive social media.

Procrastination One of the strengths of mainstream social media is that it does not actually require users to be doing anything on it beyond wasting time. With alternatives aimed at facilitating self-organisation, it would be easy to put too much focus on organisational functions such as collaboration and decision making. For an alternative platform to be successful in terms of being an effective tool for large-scale self-organisation, including encouraging more than a small tech-savvy group of activists to participate, then some of the functionality ought to be given over to what might appear to be simply wasting time. Users should be able, on such alternatives, to do all the things they do on mainstream platforms, from sharing pictures of cats, to playing interactive games. While this might seem like providing room for distractions from their core purpose, such engagement is fundamental to building self-organisation. Thinking along these lines, an alternative social media platform may need to allow for the same scope for socialising, for basically hanging out with and making friends, as both mainstream social media platforms and offline communities do. Such a platform should encourage the construction of something similar to the 'scenes' (Leach and Haunss, 2008) that have proved vital to social movement organising.

Online decision making embedded in offline structures The core purpose of online platforms of the type I am outlining here is to act as a support infrastructure for offline organising. With this is mind, any alternative digital platform ought to have a direct link between whatever decision-making functions it houses and the face-to-face decision-making procedures of the organisation using it. The precise nature of this relationship would, once again, need to be something for experimentation, but it could see online decision making subordinated to offline processes. For example, decisions made online could be subject to regular review offline. George Kokkinidis (2014) identifies a similar function in Greek workers' cooperatives, with members being able to make autonomous decisions in the day-to-day running of the organisation, but with these decisions being reviewed and potentially overruled at general assemblies. Something of this sort could be put in place to ensure that offline organising is given primacy.

Sections open to non-members As well as providing spaces for discussion and tools for organisation, alternative platforms should also act as public-facing frontages for organisations and in doing so, perhaps even allow for varying degrees of participation that permit non-members to be involved in some discussions and decision making (with other aspects of such reserved for organisation members).

Architecture for collective autonomy One of the key critiques of mainstream social media platforms is that they produce individualist subjectivities through how their various functions mould online behaviour. Addressing such critiques, through alternative social media platforms, should involve the development of architectures that are designed to move behaviour away from a commodification of the activities. Another aspect of constructing an alternative platform, could involve finding ways to support what has been referred to throughout this book as *Collective Autonomy*, that is, individual and group autonomy as constrained by overarching organisational collectivity.

Flexible engagement options Related to the previous point, concerning striking a balance between autonomy and centralisation, an alternative platform could include a function that allows individual users to manage their own engagement with groups, through providing options for users to 'step back' from specific active engagements without removing themselves entirely from a group. Such a mechanism might also help address issues of burnout and fatigue and allow individuals to take time away from intense activity and responsibility, while still maintaining their social connections.

Responsibility and commitment Another key way to achieve a balance between autonomy and organisational cohesion is to build mechanisms into an alternative digital platform that foster responsibility and commitment. This could be as simple as facilitating the linking of action points from meetings directly to the specific users that are responsible for carrying them out, with permissions automatically assigned and reminders set to reflect agreed upon deadlines.

Privacy, security and data One of the most fundamental critiques of mainstream social media that has been made in recent years has focused on how such platforms capture and monetise users' data, and how that commodified data is then used, through targeted advertising, to manipulate users, particularly with respect to their engagements in politics, such as through voting. Any alternative that aims to facilitate large-scale self-organisation and to replace mainstream platforms must address this abuse. As well as having strict controls on what user data is collected, an alternative platform should also include functions that allow for user control over what happens to their data and over how algorithms that attempt to manage noise and information overload make use of such data. Any data collected would need to be completely secure (for example, made inaccessible to government agencies) and thus not open to being used for the purpose of manipulating users.

Easy backup of information One problem often raised in relation to mainstream platforms is that users' accounts, along with any information and contacts linked to them, can be deleted without users' consent (for example if they post something the platform considers unsuitable, such as support for a group like the PKK that may be considered a terrorist organisation in many Western countries but that many on the left would view as being engaged in a legitimate liberation struggle). This may be an important function to maintain with respect to the spread misinformation or hate speech on an alternative platform, although the removal would need to be subject to democratic oversight. It ought to be made clear to all users, however, what type of actions would trigger such removal and the users of the platform must be in control of what is permitted on the platform and what is not. If groups or individual users were to decide to remove their account(s), the information contained in them should be easily exportable so that they can migrate between platforms when it suits them. The cost (financial or in terms of time and effort) of such migration should be as low as possible

Existing alternatives

Over the years, there have been several attempts made to build alternative social media platforms, where each, in different ways, has been designed to address the critiques of mainstream social media that have been discussed in this chapter. Even before social media existed as a concept, Indymedia, the radical left news website that served the alterglobalisation movement, embodied some of the interactive and participatory features of later social media platforms, allowing activists to upload their own news stories and add comments through an interface that was considerably easier to use than much of what was available on the internet. Launched in 1999, the website still operates although without the level of influence it had in the early 2000s when it was the target of several attempts at suppression by law enforcement. More recently, platforms aimed at mimicking some of positive aspects of mainstream social media's functionality have been developed, including Crabgrass, Diaspora* and Lorea, to name but three.

Crabgrass was developed by the same collective that runs the Riseup secure email provider and was aimed at facilitating: social networking, where users would get to know one another; group collaboration, where activists could organise collectively and make decisions; and intergroup networking, where different groups could come together for specific projects. It primarily operated as a groupwork platform, with forum-type mechanisms that allowed activists to share resources and collaborate. Lorea was an infrastructure that hosted a number of platforms, with N-1 being the most prominent. N-1 was based primarily in Spain and was linked to the 15M protests, having around 2,000 members before the protests and over 30,000 just after. The Lorea architecture was intended to be a 'distributed and federated nodal organization of entities with no geophysical territory' that allowed groups of activists 'to meet in assemblies, to choose delegates always revocable by the base, to connect all the sites of struggle' (Lorea, n.d.). More expansive than Crabgrass, Lorea networks allowed for customisable profile pages and dashboards, wikis, collaborative writing pads, blogs, task managers, status updates and private messaging, affiliations with and between groups and a federal structure for groups and networks. Like Crabgrass, however, Lorea did not facilitate communication beyond members of a group already using the platform. While this grew to a large number (over 40,000 across the whole architecture), it did not provide anywhere near the reach that platforms like Facebook and Twitter do. Diaspora* was designed as more of a typical social media platform, but one which gave users full control over privacy. However, it did not succeed in gaining a mass uptake of users.

Alongside less activist-oriented groupwork platforms, such as Slack and Trello, Loomio has become one of the main platforms that facilitates both general collaborative networking and participatory forms of decision making. Emerging out of the Occupy movement in New Zealand, Loomio allows groups to collaborate on projects by hosting files and facilitating discussions through a forum function. Importantly, Loomio also makes democratic decision making possible, not only through allowing for discussion but by including specific mechanisms for making proposals, providing feedback and reaching agreements, through its incorporation of some of the features of consensus decision making such as standing aside and blocking. Additionally, Loomio responds well to some of the key critiques of mainstream social media platforms, by shifting engagement away from individualised performance and towards group-based collaboration and also provides both public and private aspects for group activities, allowing for some level of access to such for non-members. While Loomio is used extensively on the radical left and in a range of other contexts, it still functions primarily as a collaborative space for already involved activists and has not enjoyed the mass appeal of a platform like Facebook (not that this has been its aim). However successful Loomio is judged to have been, the level of engagement with it highlights the problem that exists with respect to almost all alternative platforms, which is that they fail to overcome the engagement barrier that mainstream platforms have successfully overcome to a previously unimaginable degree. While even the earlier iterations of mainstream internet communications remained fairly specialist with regard to who participated, the architecture of contemporary social media has made it incredibly easy for unskilled users to play a role.

The result of the failure of any of the alternative social media platforms that have been created to date, to make the leap from a small, specialist (be that activist or technical) audience to kind the mass audience that participates on Facebook and Twitter, is that these mainstream platforms are still the primary infrastructure for much radical left organising that takes place. In spite of all their flaws, they fulfil the many of the functions required by self-organisation better than any alternative and importantly, couple this with being part of the everyday technological architecture of people's lives. Bespoke platforms have been utilised for various aspects of organising, but they have been most successful when they have focused on specific sets of tasks rather than the provision of an entire digital ecosystem. And even for highly functional, yet easy-to-use platforms, like Loomio and Slack, the barrier of having to sign up and log in to yet another platform, even for activists, has proven exceedingly difficult to overcome. App versions of these platforms that run on smartphones mitigate this, to an extent, by having users always signed in and receiving notifications that are easy to act on (rather than an email notification that can then require moving to a different platform to follow-up). In grassroots trade union organising, for example the Industrial Workers of the World, it is platforms that people are already using, like Facebook and WhatsApp (or more secure versions such as Signal), that have been key to organising workers that are not already part of left-wing circles. Perhaps, rather than producing entirely new alternative platforms, the task for radical developers is to identify suites of existing platforms that are most useful to self-organisation and to then find ways of integrating these in ways that allow for coordination (for example, by being able to send and receive WhatsApp messages from a platform like Loomio).

Undoubtedly, in the time it has taken for this book to go from its final draft to your hands, new platforms will have been introduced and perhaps already have perished. The discussion here should be viewed as an attempt to provide a broad framework for thinking about and exploring the kinds of development that would facilitate self-organisation, as inspired by the functional necessities proposed by anarchist cybernetics. Beyond this, any recommendations would, in a short space of time, likely have been overtaken and become outdated due to rapidly changing times and needs.

Conclusion

In *Designing Freedom*, Beer includes an image of what he calls 'cybernetic man [*sic*]' (1974: 69). The image, drawn by Beer in his distinctive style, shows a person seated in a chair with a series of screens in front of them and control panels on each arm of the chair. A similar image, reproduced often in published articles on cybernetics, is the photograph of the Project Cybersyn control room. Described frequently as akin to the bridge of the Starship Enterprise, it too involves a chair with control panels, surrounded by screens. For Beer, this imagining (for the Cybersyn control room was only ever a mock-up) of an individual seated comfortably, able to review information from various sources in real time and to react to it using the controls in the chair, was a depiction of how he envisaged the individual fitting into an effective self-organised system. Constantly connected to a communication network with information running through it, people could act in real time to respond to change as it happened. The text beneath the image has the individual making a series of demands of the technology surrounding them, asking to know more about a news item, to pull up some historical information, to explain a scientific term, update a tax record, send a notification to a friend about a telecommunicated chess game, and so on.

Move forward almost half a century and Beer's vision of social organisation managed collectively by individuals connected through real-time technological infrastructures is, in many ways, realised not in anything like the Project Cybersyn control room but in the smartphones most of us carry in our pockets. Through these devices, we receive immediate updates about the various things happening in the world that are of concern to us, and the simple user-interface of many apps allow us to respond instantly. The cybernetic person in Beer's sketch has been brought into being, but in a much more mobile way than he originally envisaged. News apps and Twitter allow us to stay on top of news, Wikipedia provides knowledge at our fingertips, online banking allows us to keep on top of our finances and various apps let us play games with people in every corner of the world, with notifications informing us when it's our next turn. Beer completes his, all too accurate, vision of the future with a nod to some of the concerns around privacy and data discussed in this chapter: 'AND DON'T TELL ANYONE ELSE UNLESS I SAY SO'. The user is in control.

Social media platforms, in so far as they facilitate interactive communication and organisation, have the potential to play a central role in anarchist cybernetics and thus anarchist (self-) organisation more broadly. Crucially, though, we have to rethink how social media function and how we engage with them as users. Mainstream platforms, such as Twitter and Facebook, have been subject to a range of critiques, four of which – around privacy and the use of data, political economy, weak ties and subjectivity – I have addressed in this chapter. As well as responding to these critiques, the discussion here, of how alternative platforms might function, has also examined some of the key features that would allow an alternative social media platform to operate effectively to support self-organisation. As I mentioned at the start of this chapter, lacking any technical knowledge, my aim here has not been to provide a detailed account of how such an alternative could be built but, rather, through drawing on how anarchist cybernetics understands control and communication, to highlight some potential parameters within which alternatives could be developed.

In line with anarchist cybernetics' commitment to prefiguration, any such efforts to develop alternative social media platforms and apply them to anarchist self-organisation need to be democratic, participatory and experimental processes. It is those involved in their creation that will need to determine what specific functions are required to support their desired forms of self-organisation, with attention to what is needed in the specific niches they are concerned and involved with. What this account of alternative platforms aims to do, as with the purpose of Beer's Viable System Model, is aid these contextualised processes through provision of a discussion of the broader concerns as to how alternatives might perform and what roles they might fulfil.

8

Organising Radical Left Populism

In the preceding chapters, I have tried to outline how anarchist cybernetics – defined as a meeting of anarchist theories and practices of self-organisation, on the one hand, and Stafford Beer's organisational cybernetics, on the other – is well positioned to provide insights into and possible solutions to some of the complex problems facing radical left organisation. Primarily through the example of the Occupy movement, the book has explored how taking a cybernetics perspective with respect to issues of organisation can help those involved in radical politics better understand what happens when participatory and democratic self-organisation works as it should and how such organisation might be achieved. Rather than providing a model of organisation, a blueprint that can be followed to ensure success, the book and anarchist cybernetics more generally are intended, like Beer's cybernetics itself, as tools to aid those engaging in organising to identify and address problems that commonly arise. By focusing on control (understood as self-organisation) and communication, the discussion throughout has been focused on how particular functions and mechanisms of organising operate in ways that enable organisations to respond to complexity and change, while achieving the goals they set themselves. Anarchist cybernetics does not *prescribe* how such organisations should be structured but instead foregrounds some of the necessary functions of self-organisation and suggests how these can be realised, without constructing and reinforcing structural hierarchies. The three central concepts that underpin this framework are self-organisation, functional hierarchy and many-to-many communication.

Self-organisation is a foundational concept that is common to both anarchist politics and cybernetics and has been identified by authors, such as Colin Ward and John McEwan, as a key area of shared interest about which the two traditions can fruitfully inform one another (as outlined at length in Chapter 3). Within anarchism, self-organisation is understood to refer to how groups of people are able to come together as a collective entity, make decisions and act purposefully, without the need for bosses hierarchically above them issuing orders and having oversight over the actions of the whole collective. In cybernetics, self-organisation is a more technical concept and is used to describe how systems – mechanical, electronic, biological or indeed social – have the potential to regulate their behaviour in line with set goals. Cybernetics, derived from the Ancient Greek word *kybernetes*, involves how systems can steer themselves and avoid being taken off course by changes in their environment. As I mentioned earlier in the book, one of the most ubiquitous examples used in cybernetics is that of the thermostat: it regulates the temperature of the room by modifying the output of the heater or air-conditioning unit. The three parts (thermostat, room with temperature and heater) form a single system that has a goal (a specific temperature) and can self-organise through feedback to achieve that goal in response to changes in the environment around it (the varying temperature outside that heats or cools the room).

For cybernetics, systems that function in this way are self-organising, but only as viewed from a certain perspective. In the example just given, if we zoom out from the system, it is clear that someone has to set the thermostat and so in that sense the system is still being directed from the outside. For social systems, however, this self-organisation process can be realised in a much more direct way, by people in an organisation coming together and regulating their behaviour collectively. The meeting of anarchism and cybernetics, in self-organising social systems, depends on those systems being both goal-directed and goal-forming; in other words, they are able to both navigate complexity while achieving their goals as well as deciding on what those goals should be through similarly self-organised practices. As Chapters 4 and 5 highlighted, anarchist organisation has several forms of decision-making practice that, in different ways, aim to find a balance between the autonomy that various parts of organisations require to respond to complexity and change and the cohesion that the organisation as a whole demands, which involves having collectively agreed overarching goals or strategies that limit the tactical autonomy each of the various parts of the organisation possesses. Consensus decision making is one such mechanism for reaching decisions, through which this balance can be reached and, when combined with a reflexive, prefigurative politics, enables the strategic functions of the organisation to also be subject to participatory and democratic control. It is through such processes for decision making, implemented in these ways, that anarchist organisation can meet the conditions identified by anarchist cybernetics as necessary for effective self-organisation. To fully achieve this, however, attention also has to be paid to communication – specifically to how the infrastructures of self-organisation support appropriate forms of communication and vice versa.

As well as Beer's work on cybernetics being of particular interest in this discussion of anarchist cybernetics, conversation theory, developed by Beer's fellow cybernetician Gordon Pask, is also important. In cybernetics, organisation is fundamentally an issue of communication. The different parts of a system or organisation are linked, in a network, by lines of communication. Without such communicative links, self-organisation is not be possible. As was shown in Chapters 6 and 7, there is a need to recognise that certain forms of communication will be more supportive of self-organisation than others. For Pask, conversation is the key way in which communication functions in self-organised systems. Such a notion of conversation involves communication between equals, in which information is shared and in which there is no one dictating to anyone else. When done well, these types of conversation reflect the horizontal nature of self-organisation. This emphasis on interactive, conversational communication is also reflected in the conception of many-to-many communication that is discussed in this book, where networks operate in ways that allow for anyone in a network to communicate and share information with anyone else in the network. As was made clear during the 2011 uprisings, the technological infrastructures of communication, such as social media platforms, are vital to the effectiveness of both conversation and many-to-many communication in the context of self-organisation. The discussion here has tried to point out the various functions that these technologies and the communication networks they foster need to include. This can involve, for instance, shaping how noise is experienced and produced in communication processes as well as defining the kind of alternative social media platforms that are best suited to achieving the tasks that anarchist cybernetics foregrounds as vital.

Radical politics since 2011 and the electoral turn

By the time this book is being read, most likely a decade or more will have passed since the uprisings of 2011 and the contemporary horizon of radical politics looks very different from how it did back then. One by one, the prefigurative promise of occupations across the world, to build a new form of democracy in the shell of the old, failed to be realised. In Spain the 15M movement's encampments were cleared and destroyed by riot police. Similar coordinated police action saw Occupy camps in the US and elsewhere also evicted and dismantled. Most tragic of all was the fate that was in store for the Arab Spring. In Egypt, where the Tahrir Square occupation had been a model for movements around the globe, a dictatorship was overthrown only to be eventually replaced by a government run by the military, under which even the basic requirements of liberal democracy, never mind radical visions of revolution, were lacking. In Libya, the toppling of Ghaddafi's regime witnessed fighting break out between rival factions. This same dynamic emerged in Syria, although with the government retaining power over much of the country and civil war erupting between different rebel groups, government forces, religious extremists in the form of ISIS and, in the North, the Kurdish separatist movement. While the autonomous region carved out in Northern Syria by Kurdish and allied militias, in a region called Rojava, still holds some of the promise of participatory and democratic self-organisation (in spite of Turkish military invasion that has led to some parts of the area being occupied), elsewhere the ruptures caused by the 2011 uprisings have not led to a realisation of radically democratic governance on any larger scale than already existed in the various left-wing groups that had developed these practices over the previous decades.

In Europe and the US, rather than radical politics developing in a linear fashion from 2011, continuing to have a central focus on the occupation of public space and defining areas of autonomy and self-organisation, the political drive and momentum of the 2011 uprisings has shifted from a focus on social movement organising to a hybrid form of politics involving both mass mobilisation and a strategy of standing in elections. For many of the activists involved in Occupy, for example, engagement in the systems and institutions of liberal democracy was the antithesis of their politics. The slogan 'this is what democracy looks like' contrasted the dominant forms of so-called representative democracy (viewed as democratic in name only) with the genuine and substantive 'real' democracy of Occupy's general assembly and related participatory structures. And yet, the focus of large sections of the radical left in the decade since has been on supporting and campaigning for political parties, in some cases through support for specific long-standing veterans of representative systems, such as Bernie Sanders in the US and Jeremy Corbyn in the UK. Greece was perhaps the first place where such a strong electoral turn was witnessed, with the rise of the Syriza party, which succeeded in capturing public resentment against the austerity programme forced on the country by the European Commission, the IMF and the European Central Bank and directing this into electoral politics. Doing so involved taking much of the anger that had been expressed in mass street mobilisations and channelling it into electing a party that was viewed by many at the time as embodying a radical social democratic politics. The Podemos party in Spain charted a similar course, by successfully transforming much of the energy of the 2011 movement into electoral politics. Keir Milburn quotes John McDonnell, the UK Labour Party politician and former Shadow Chancellor, in defining this strategy as working 'in and against' the state (Milburn, 2019: 102; McDonnell is here rearticulating the strategy first set out in the pamphlet 'In and Against the State' (London Edinburgh Weekend Return Group, 1979) and restated by John Holloway (2016), one of the authors of that pamphlet, as 'in, against and beyond capitalism').

In his book *Generation Left*, Milburn argues that the identification of the general assembly with real democracy was an error of judgement on the part of movements like Occupy. 'Assemblyism', as he calls it, 'mistook consensus assemblies, which had emerged from quite specific circumstances and inheritances, for a new universal model of democracy, which at the very least prefigured the post-capitalist society to come' (2019: 75–6). Paolo Gerbaudo makes a similar point, when characterising the view of the protest camps as prefigurative autonomous communes as 'counterproductive' and '[u]nable to imagine more broadly beyond that which could be immediately touched or experienced' (2017: 179). The electoral turn, and the move away from creating autonomous zones of prefigurative democracy to capturing and reforming the institutions of the state, can be viewed as a development of the radical politics of the 2011 uprisings, as a response to the limitations those movements experienced. Milburn writes that '[r]ather than seeing the general assemblies, and so the movements of 2011, as a failure because they reached their limits of scalability, we should see them as a necessary moment in the emergence of a new political generation' (2019: 77). The electoral turn is, he goes on to note, 'the continuation of the same project through a different mode of politics' (2019: 87). Gerbaudo too considers the 2011 uprisings as 'a fundamental historical turning and a foundational development for a new wave of progressive politics' (2017: 24).

For these authors, and others, an effective response to the demise of the 2011 uprisings and the participatory democratic form of organisation they embodied, should move with and beyond them, taking their radical politics to (for many involved) the new terrain of elections, mass political parties and the capture and reshaping of state power. In the context of this strategic turn, how might the participatory democratic practice of movements like Occupy be retained? How can an engagement with electoral politics and institutions, like political parties and parliaments, remain consistent with a prefigurative politics that not only aims for a society devoid of domination but that attempts to realise that goal in the present? For anarchists, despite the failure of the 2011 movements to strengthen and expand the islands of democracy they had created, their systemic critique of institutions, like political parties and mainstream trade unions, still stands. Based on top-down modes of organisation where leaders (albeit elected ones) make key strategic decisions and members throughout the organisation enact those decisions, these institutions are the antithesis of anarchism's prefigurative drive and, indeed, of the way participatory and democratic self-organisation has been framed throughout this book. In attempting to resolve this contradiction between the electoral turn and a commitment to participatory and democratic decision making, two key issues need to be addressed: first, how can anarchist prefigurative politics sit side-by-side with the new left-wing populism of this electoral turn; second, what does this mean for how political institutions are structured?

Anarchism and radical left populism

Gerbaudo (2017) argues that an essential aspect of the move away from the prefigurative politics of the movement of the squares is engagement with a populism that is rooted in an inclusive notion of the citizen. Populisms of the right are founded on an exclusionary imagining of 'the people'. For instance, the right-wing populism that has coalesced around the UK's exit from the European Union has involved the exclusion of immigrants and even those born in the UK but considered 'traitors', such as those wanting to reverse the Brexit vote or simply uphold existing arrangements of parliamentary government. In contrast, the populism Gerbaudo identifies in the 2011 movements and as underlying their subsequent turn towards electoral politics is based on a construction of 'the people' as citizens with corresponding rights and responsibilities in a democratic system and as defined in opposition to corrupt political and financial elites. One of the most enduring aspects of the 2011 uprisings was their formulation of the people versus the bankers and the politicians, expressed in Occupy as the 99% versus the 1% and in similar terms elsewhere. As Gerbaudo notes (2017: 72), such a framing of the people, as constituting those in opposition to the elites, is not alien to anarchism (see also Gordon (2017) on the relationship and distinction between anarchism's framing of 'the people' and the nationalism common to both right-wing and many left-wing forms of populism).

Rather than conceiving of prefigurative anarchist political practice as inevitably in stark opposition to the idea of popular sovereignty that leads to a citizen-based populism and a focus on electoral politics, an approach that draws on recent work on anarchist constitutionalising might usefully shed light on how participatory and democratic self-organisation can move in and against existing institutions, without sacrificing its critique of hierarchy and domination. In contrast to anarchists such as Goldman (1940) and Graeber (2013) who view constitutional politics and anarchism as at odds with one another, anarchist constitutionalising (Kinna and Prichard, 2019; Kinna et al., 2019; Seeds for Change and Anarchy Rules, 2018) recognises the importance of the core features of any constitutional arrangement and tries to show how these can be realised in ways that eschew the domination inherent in other forms of governance. Like cybernetics with its focus on necessary functions, in many ways, it identifies functions of constitutionalising that need to be fulfilled in the contexts of contemporary societies, but detaches these from typical constitutional arrangements, such as representative democracy. In an attempt to show that 'a grass-roots, post-statist constitutional politics' is possible (Kinna et al., 2019: 359), anarchist constitutionalising draws on four core features of constitutional politics: 1) declarative principles; 2) institutions; 3) decision-making procedures; and 4) formal and informal rules. These very features were witnessed in the Occupy camps; in the declarations and statements they produced, in their structural components such as the general assembly and the spokes-council, in their consensus and modified-consensus decision making and with respect to the agreed obligations of camp participants. Beyond Occupy and beyond the uprisings of 2011, however, this anarchist approach to constitutional politics, by replicating vital functions of constitutional politics while rejecting hierarchies of domination, can be seen to more broadly point towards how a consistently anarchist populist politics could operate.

One example that shows the potential of this kind of anarchist constitutional politics as a frame for analysing and understanding how participatory democratic process can sit in and against institutions of the state is the attempt in Iceland to write a new national constitution. Often missed out from narratives of the 2011 uprisings and the events that followed, Iceland's 'pots and pans revolution' – so named because of the noise protestors made by banging kitchen implements together when they surrounded the parliament in Reykjavík – is, like Occupy, 15M and the Arab Spring, rooted in the financial crash of 2008 and was similarly a revolt against what was viewed as corrupt political and financial governance. Happening almost immediately after the crash in 2008, mass protests towards the end of that year forced the centre-right government from power, with new elections installing a government led by social democrats for the first time in Iceland's history. Among other measures aimed at reasserting the sovereignty of the people over control by elites, the new government began a process of having Iceland's constitution rewritten. The existing constitution was hastily drawn up to cement Iceland's independence from Denmark after World War Two and basically replicated the Danish constitution, doing little more than changing references to the Danish monarch to references to the Icelandic president. Of particular interest, for this discussion of anarchist constitutionalising was how the new constitution was to be written. As Helen Landemore comments (2015: 168), the process involved '(i) direct popular participation at various stages of the process, (ii) elements of descriptive representativeness where direct participation wasn't possible, and (iii) transparency.'

In practice, a citizen's assembly was established, with 1,000 Icelanders being randomly selected to discuss and agree on the core values of Iceland as a nation. A Constitutional Council of 25 people (none of whom were allowed to be serving politicians or civil servants) was then elected to do the actual work of writing the constitution, based on these values. Drafts were posted online and through social media and other channels members of the public were able to observe and comment on the writing process. While this attempt at democratising constitution writing in a radical way has been critiqued on various grounds (for example, Ólafsson, 2016), it suggests how constitutional politics can be done in ways that converge with how anarchist cybernetics has articulated participatory and democratic self-organisation. First, this can be seen as an attempt at making the grand strategic function open to democratic participation, at a scale far above anything attempted by Occupy or related movements. Second, it stands as an example of the kind of non-statist constitutionalising outlined earlier in this section. Importantly, the process began with a population rising up to throw a government out of office. While they certainly did not do away with the state, the initiative in the constitutionalising process shifted from the state as the sovereign to the people as sovereign. This anarchist cybernetic understanding can also help explain, at least in part, why the process ultimately failed.

Once the new constitution was drafted it was put to the population in a referendum and accepted with a significant majority voting in favour. Before it could be ratified by parliament, however, new elections took place and the centre-right regained power. Following this turn of events, the draft constitution that had been approved in the referendum was never implemented. To this day, serious attempts are still being made to have all or some of the new constitution adopted, but the ground has shifted significantly, with, it could be argued, the state regaining the initiative and control over the constitutionalising process. One of the things this illustrates is the potential for prefigurative, participatory forms of democracy to gain public support in moments of crises when the state is weakened and movements are able to assert control and shape constitutional arrangements. It also, of course, illustrates likely threats to such processes. The case of Iceland's attempt at constitutional revolution suggests that when the state is weakened, participatory democracy can grow from the immediate confines of the public square to much larger and geographically spread out communities. If John Holloway's account of the 'cracks' in capitalism (2010) can be used to explain how myriad experiments in radically alternative ways of living can thrive inside seemingly dominant systems, perhaps this example from Iceland shows how cracks in the state can be the site of more unified experiments in mass forms of participatory democracy. Indeed, in a similar vein, Jón Gunnar Bernburg (2016) has deployed the concept of 'breakdown' to help explain the moment of democratic possibility in Iceland. The populist 'people', it could be suggested, is able to act through processes that go beyond the system of representative democracy correlative to the political party, processes that involve direct participation in governance. As such, the model of society prefigured in the 2011 uprisings is writ large.

In Syria, a country still in the grip of conflict almost a decade after the revolution against the Assad regime began, we also see examples of participatory democracy and mutual aid, as self-organised communities carve out spaces of autonomy. In the North of the country, inspired by the democratic confederalism of Abdullah Ocalan (which was itself inspired by Bookchin's social ecology), a territory known as Rojava has put anarchistic democratic organisation into practice on a large scale. Of central importance is how the Movement for a Democratic Society (TEV-DEM) facilitates coordination between autonomous communes. As Yagmur Savran writes (2016: 8), 'TEV-DEM is leading the social coordination of the three cantons in Rojava and has assisted cities, villages and towns to create a communal form of democracy based on a bottom-up approach to politics to transfer power from the state into the hands of the people.' Delegates from small local units are sent to higher levels in the federation, much like the spokes-council model Occupy tried to implement. In spite of constant threat from ISIS and the Turkish state, and in a complex relationship with the US which at times has provided military support, Rojava has maintained participatory democratic structures of governance and a commitment to feminism and ethnic inclusivity. Kinna calls this 'a sweeping experiment in anarchy' (2019: 246) that demonstrates the influence of anarchism beyond those movements that explicitly self-identify with anarchism ideologically (Yassin-Kassab and Al-Shami (2018) discuss similar revolutionary democratic forms of organisation elsewhere in Syria). The federalist model of Rojava suggests how state-like coordinating functions can be replicated without the domination that states structurally impose and reproduce.

Operating in the context of the state (in Iceland, the production of a national constitution, and in Rojava, the creation of a central state-like body), these examples suggest that radical politics has the potential, as McDonnell puts it, to work 'in and against the state'. As Graham Jones argues, while 'the state – and indeed all dominating bodies – will not wither away of its own accord [...] parts of the state should be progressively disempowered from within' (2018: 121). Interestingly, Jones draws explicitly on Beer's work, in particular his book *Designing Freedom*, in proposing a radical left strategy built around fundamentally altering the way the state operates so as to make autonomy and self-organisation possible. Specifically, in relation to the issue of complexity and Ashby's Law of Requisite Variety (discussed in Chapter 3), he writes:

> An alternative means of expanding internal complexity would be decentralization of power, allowing multiple autonomous centres of sensing and adaptation guided by local knowledge. The centralized state is fundamentally incapable of surmounting our current complex crises, and must be replaced with a more participatory, decentralized and adaptable structure in order for us to survive. (Jones, 2018: 90)

The examples of Iceland's democratic constitutionalising and the autonomous communes of Rojava serve to suggest how the process of anarchist cybernetics might operate at a scale far beyond the general assemblies and other bodies that comprised Occupy and other movements. Importantly, linking this back to the discussion of Beer's Viable System Model, these case studies also point towards ways in which Salvador Allende's exclamation of 'at last, the people' when looking at System Five in the VSM can be realised in practical ways that go beyond representative democracy. If radical left populism is about putting the people in control, anarchist cybernetics may provide a framework for showing how that can be made possible.

Coexistence and hybridity

If anarchist cybernetics is to provide an organising framework for radical left populism, following the shift from social movement organising to a hybrid strategy of acting in and against state institutions, one of the key challenges will be to show how the balance between autonomy and centralisation can be articulated in these circumstances. In the run-up to the Scottish independence referendum in 2014, political philosopher Richard Gunn spoke to this tension, in distinguishing between interaction and institution: 'Institutions have a built-in, hierarchical dynamic: they obey an iron law of oligarchy that generates role definitions – role definitions which claim authority and cluster together at the top. By contrast, interaction which follows its own inner logic is unrestricted and in principle free' (Gunn, 2014).

Elsewhere, writing with R.C. Smith and Adrian Wilding on the nature of interaction, Gunn adds:

> An analogy may be drawn with conversation: a 'good' discussion follows its subject-matter wherever it leads. It *gives its law to itself.* So it is, we suggest, with interaction. Interaction *which is truly interaction* has an unstructured character. That is to say, it is not confined to previously-established channels. It decides its own patterns and consults itself. (Gunn et al., 2015, emphasis in original)

Interestingly, in framing definitions of and relationships between interaction and institution in this way, Gunn and his co-authors draw (perhaps unknowingly) on two core aspects of cybernetics that are central to anarchist cybernetics: roles in organisations and the idea of conversation.

As the discussion of functional hierarchy, as contrasted with structural or anatomical hierarchy, in this book has suggested, the way functions and roles in anarchist and related organisational forms are arranged will differ considerably. As Gunn points out, in what he calls *institutions* and what I have referred to here as the organisational functions of *structural hierarchies*, specific roles will be ordered vertically and in a top–down command structure. In this case, to the extent that this organisational form is able to operate effectively, the functions identified in Beer's Viable System Model will be reflected in a hierarchical structure where separate layers of personnel will take on different roles. For example, workers will be subordinated to managers, who in turn will be subordinated to a board of executives. With respect to political organisation, this is the type of structure that is present in political parties, traditional trade unions and related organisations, with members and activists at the bottom of the hierarchy, receiving orders from local and regional officials, who in turn receive orders from national executives. Ultimately, the functions of organisation are arranged in ways that involve the leadership at the top taking on strategic and grand strategic functions, with those at the bottom of the hierarchy potentially possessing some tactical autonomy but essentially having no control over the functional constraints on that autonomy. In an election campaign or in trade union organising, activists follow the orders of those above them in the chain of command. While those in structurally higher positions of authority may be elected, the opportunity for participation in functionally higher roles is limited.

To transform this organisational dynamic and shift the structural hierarchies of institutions towards functional hierarchy of the sort consistent with anarchist organising principles, as Gunn argues, they need to be made to operate as conversations. Reading this in the contexts of the discussion of communication, and in particular Pask's work on conversation theory, in this book means restructuring these institutions in ways that ensure that horizontal communication is prioritised. Hierarchies of command are fundamentally at odds with how conversations function. While a conversation might have a facilitator and rules, these operate in ways that are intended not to dictate the content or form of the conversation but to guide it so that the participants are able to communicate effectively. The challenge for bringing together, as Gunn phrases it, interaction and institution, or as I have expressed it here, functional and structure hierarchies, is to identify how these opposing dynamics can inhabit the same organisational space. How can participatory and democratic functional role arrangements sit alongside structural hierarchies of command? How can conversation be maintained in environments where communication is reduced to issuing orders? To navigate these oppositions, two possibilities present themselves: first, these differing organisational approaches can work independently of one another but towards shared goals; second, a hybrid form of organisation can be created that attempts to incorporate both approaches and mitigate for their opposition.

Since 2011, both approaches have been witnessed, with neither emerging as an obvious solution for reconciling this opposition once and for all. In political parties, like Podemos in Spain or the Pirate Party in Iceland, participatory structures utilising social media–type platforms have at times allowed for members to have more direct control over party strategy than has ever previously been the case in parliamentary politics, but these developments have not been met with the same level of enthusiasm and mobilisation as the 2011 uprisings suggested was possible. In the UK Labour Party, while the election of Jeremy Corbyn as leader in 2015 and the party's gains in the 2017 general election was made possible due to a mass mobilisation of activists, the extent to which this materialised in terms of an effective structure of participation at all levels of the party, or even with regard to Momentum, a more radical platform within the Labour Party, is limited. In Scotland, while the Scottish National Party benefitted from the mobilisation of tens of thousands of activists during the campaign for independence in 2014, both in terms of increased membership and campaigning potential during the 2015 UK general election, this has not translated into a change in the centralised decision making structure of the party.

In these cases, that are representative of both the electoral turn in radical politics and of a radical left populism, the horizontal, participatory nature of mass mobilisations has not effectively been combined with existing hierarchical structures, either in the coexistence model, as evidenced by the cases of the UK Labour Party or the Scottish National Party, or in the hybrid model, of Podemos and the Pirate Party.

A strategic anarchism

Some aspects of these examples may, of course, seem at odds with anarchist politics. While there were moves among a small number of anarchist activists to join the Labour Party or otherwise support Jeremy Corbyn's leadership in 2015 and vocal support for Corbyn's Labour from high-profile anarchists such as David Graeber and Alan Moore at the 2019 general election, the electoral turn in radical politics has also been met with a more anticipated scepticism by other anarchists and those whose analysis of domination places political parties in the frame as one of the main historical structures of top-down control. With both Corbyn's tenure as Labour Party leader and Bernie Sanders' campaign for the Democratic Party presidential nomination both coming to an end in the same month, April 2020, and the ensuing debate over the structural bias against progressive, left-wing politics in these party institutions, there is a sense in which the scepticism of the electoral turn has been vindicated. It was precisely a disagreement over forming political parties (and the associated strategy of seizing state power) that caused the split in the First International between the Marxists and the anarchists. Is the attempt at bringing the interactive nature of horizontal movements together with the institutional structure of vertical parties and similar organisations like trade unions something that will only ever result in the institution overwhelming the interaction, thus reproducing the structural hierarchy and command and control system anarchists oppose? Tentatively, I want to suggest that no, it need not inevitably lead to this conclusion. By not only working with, but also against, structurally hierarchical institutions like parties, to reshape them from within, anarchism can play a constructive role in these recent developments within radical left politics, even if the path towards such a reshaping may seem less obvious in the wake of the rout of the radical left in the Labour Party and the Democratic Party in 2020. In the spirit of prefiguration, however, such a process of constructive engagement involves experimentation and a constant reassessment of strategy and tactics designed to contest control in this new terrain. If the strategies centred around Corbyn and Sanders have been stymied, then sober analysis is required to determine what went wrong and why, and to identify what avenues are left open or might be opened in the future.

More importantly, however, this shift to an anarchism that works in and against the institutions of the state, may require a change in how anarchists approach questions of political power. One of the key legacies of the alterglobalisation movement is a rejection of hegemonic politics in favour of a politics built around a proliferation of autonomous affinity groups. Richard Day, the author most closely associated with this shift, characterised this as a 'displacement of the hegemony of hegemony by an affinity for affinity' (2005: 9). Hegemony, as the concept has been used in radical theory, going back to the work of Antonio Gramsci, concerns the ideological dominance of a particular politics. Capitalism can be said to have hegemony over our lives, in the sense that it shapes our central understandings of the world and how we interact with one another. This is not limited to the fact that under capitalism we are forced to sell our labour to survive, but that the logic of capitalism works its way into all social interaction. Counter-hegemonic politics, then, is an attempt to displace one hegemony with another; in other words, to replace capitalist hegemony with a communist or socialist one:

> This might mean a defence of the welfare state in the global North, or a continuation of the battle to enjoy its benefits for the first time in the global South. Or it might mean attempting to establish a *different kind* of global hegemony, one that works from 'below' rather than from 'above'. (Day, 2005: 8, emphasis in original)

For Day, this approach makes the mistake of attempting to replace one overarching system of domination with another; perhaps it would be less destructive of life in all its forms, but, so the argument goes, it would still be an attempt to shape the world in a certain way, from above and with little concern for autonomy and difference. Day instead notes the emergence of an 'affinity for affinity', an approach that adopts dispersed and diverse tactics and strategies that are 'non-universalizing, non-hierarchical [and] non-coercive' (2005: 8).

It is support for this type of approach that can be seen as underpinning the initial enthusiasm for the 2011 uprisings among anarchists and similar radical leftists. Rather than attempting to take control of the state through elections or other means, and bring about reform and indeed transformation that way, these movements were seen to be carving out spaces of autonomy within territories governed by the state. The hope was that, eventually, these autonomous zones would link up and federate, and through doing so lead to the state and other forces of domination withering away, not through centrally managed policies but through their increasing irrelevance to people's lives. The failure of this strategy, I would suggest, calls on those on the radical left to rethink the affinity for affinity approach to social movement organising and reappraise the counter-hegemonic strategy that the alterglobalisation movement abandoned. This is perhaps what is being witnessing in the electoral turn: an imperfect and perhaps impossible attempt at a return to a radical left counter-hegemonic politics. Examples, such as the participatory constitutionalising process in Iceland and the federated communes of Rojava, may point towards processes whereby radical and even anarchist politics can be counter-hegemonic without being appropriated by the logics of domination that are bound up in the state. If anarchist cybernetics is to be useful now, and in the future, it is in such realms of possibility that it might be applied. By identifying the functions of participatory and democratic self-organisation, anarchist cybernetics helps show not only how spaces of autonomy like the Occupy camps were run; it also suggests how these functions might be replicated on a larger scale, at a higher level of federation or recursion. By separating organisational function from organisation form, anarchist cybernetics highlights how anarchist and radical left organising can maintain its commitment to self-organisation in new political terrains and, crucially, points towards how institutions can be reshaped to create space for genuinely democratic participation.

References

Aguilera, M., Morer, I., Barandiaran, X.E. and Bedia, M.G. (2013) 'Quantifying Political Self-Organization in Social Media. Fractal Patterns in the Spanish 15M Movement on Twitter', [online] available from: https://maguilera0.files.wordpress.com/2012/11/main.pdf [accessed 10 September 2019].

Ampère, A.-M. (1843) *Essai sur la philosophie des sciences, Bd. 2,* Paris: Chez Bachelier.

Ashby, W.R. (1956) *An Introduction to Cybernetics,* London and New York: Methuen.

Ashby, W.R. ([1958] 2003) 'Requisite Variety and its Implications for the Control of Complex Systems', in G. Midgley (ed.) *Systems Thinking. Volume 1. General Systems Theory, Cybernetics and Complexity,* London: Sage, pp. 352–64.

Ashby, W.R. (1962) 'Principles of the Self-Organizing System', in H. von Foerster and G.W. Zopf Jr. (eds) *Principles of Self-Organization. Transactions of the University of Illinois Symposium,* London: Pergamon Press, pp. 255–78.

Baarts, C. (2009) 'Collective Individualism: The Informal and Emergent Dynamics of Practising Safety in a High-Risk Work Environment', *Construction Management and Economics,* 27(10): 949–57.

Baker, S.A. (2011) 'The Mediated Crowd: New Social Media and New Forms of Rioting', *Sociological Research Online,* 16(4).

Bakunin, M. (1866) 'Revolutionary Catechism', [online] available from: https://theanarchistlibrary.org/library/michail-bakunin-revolutionary-catechism [accessed 20 September 2019].

Bakunin, M. (1871) 'The Paris Commune and the Idea of the State', [online] available from: https://theanarchistlibrary.org/library/michail-bakunin-the-paris-commune-and-the-idea-of-the-state [accessed 07 September 2019].

Baltazar, A.P. (2007) 'Towards a Virtual Architecture: Pushing Cybernetics from Government to Anarchy', *Kybernetes,* 36(9/10): 1238–54.

Baran, P. (1962) 'On Distributed Communications Networks', [online] available from: www.rand.org/content/dam/rand/pubs/papers/2005/P2626.pdf [accessed 20 September 2019].

Barrington-Bush, L. (2013) *Anarchists in the Boardroom. How Social Media and Social Movements Can Help Your Organisation to be More Like People.* London: More Like People.

Beer, S. (1967) *Cybernetics and Management* (2nd edn), London: The English Universities Press.

Beer, S. (1972a) 'Five Principles for the People for Good Government', [online] available from: http://digitool.jmu.ac.uk:1801/webclient/DeliveryManager?application=DIGITOOL-3&owner=resourcediscovery&custom_att_2=simple_viewer&pid=15986 [accessed 08 September 2019].

Beer, S. (1972b) 'One Year of (Relative) Solitude. The Second Level of Recursion', [online] available from: http://digitool.jmu.ac.uk:1801/webclient/DeliveryManager?application=DIGITOOL-3&owner=resourcediscovery&custom_att_2=simple_viewer&pid=15983 [accessed 08 September 2019].

Beer, S. (1973) 'Fanfare for Effective Freedom. Cybernetics Praxis in Government', [online] available from: www.kybernetik.ch/dwn/Fanfare_for_Freedom.pdf [accessed 08 September 2019].

Beer, S. (1974) *Designing Freedom*, Chichester: John Wiley & Sons.

Beer, S. ([1974] 1994) 'Cybernetics of National Development', in R. Harnden and A. Leonard (eds) *How Many Grapes Went into the Wine. Stafford Beer and the Art and Science of Holistic Management*, Chichester: John Wiley & Sons, pp. 317–40.

Beer, S. ([1975] 1994) *Platform for Change*, Chichester: John Wiley & Sons.

Beer, S. ([1975] 2009) 'Laws of Anarchy', in D. Whitaker (ed.) *Think Before You Think. Social Complexity and Knowledge of Knowing*, Oxon: Wavestone Press, pp. 23–35.

Beer, S. ([1979] 1994) *Heart of the Enterprise*, Chichester: John Wiley & Sons.

Beer, S. ([1981] 1994) *Brain of the Firm* (2nd edn), Chichester: John Wiley & Sons.

Beer, S. (1985) *Diagnosing the System for Organisations*, Chichester: John Wiley & Sons.

Beer, S. ([1987] 1994) 'Holism and the Frou-Frou Slander', in R. Harnden and A. Leonard (eds) *How Many Grapes Went into the Wine. Stafford Beer and the Art and Science of Holistic Management*, Chichester: John Wiley & Sons, pp. 13–23.

Beer, S. (1994) *Beyond Dispute. The Invention of Team Syntegrity*, Chichester: John Wiley & Sons.

Beer, V. and Leonard, A. (2019) *Stafford Beer. The Father of Management Cybernetics*, Switzerland: Fondation Oroborus.

Bell, D.M. (2014) 'Improvisation as Anarchist Organisation', *ephemera: theory & politics in organization*, 14(4): 1009–30.

Bernburg, J.G. (2016) *Economic Crisis and Mass Protest: The Pots and Pans Revolution in Iceland*, London: Routledge.

Beverungen, A., Böhm, S. and Land, C. (2015) 'Free Labour, Social Media, Management: Challenging Marxist Organization Studies', *Organization Studies*, 36(4): 473–89.

Beyes, T.P. (2005) 'Observing Observers. Von Foerster, Luhmann, and Management Thinking', *Kybernetes*, 34(3/4): 448–59.

Boggs, C. (1977) 'Marxism, Prefigurative Communism and the Problem of Workers' Control', *Radical America*, 11(6)/12(1): 99–122.

Bookchin, M. (1995) *Social Anarchism or Lifestyle Anarchism. An Unbridgeable Chasm*, Edinburgh and Oakland: AK Press.

Boyd, J. (2005) 'Patterns of Conflict', [online] available from: www.projectwhitehorse.com/pdfs/boyd/patterns%20of%20conflict.pdf [accessed 07 September 2019].

Bray M. (2013) *Translating Anarchy: The Anarchism of Occupy Wall Street*, Winchester: Zero Books.

Breines, W. (1980) 'Community and Organization: The New Left and Michels' 'Iron Law'', *Social Problems*, 27(4): 419–29.

Cadwalladr, C. (2017) 'The Great British Brexit Robbery: How Our Democracy was Hijacked', *The Guardian*, [online] available from: www.theguardian.com/technology/2017/may/07/the-great-british-brexit-robbery-hijacked-democracy [accessed 28 September 2019].

Carby, Hazel (1982) 'White Woman Listen! Black Feminism and the Boundaries of Sisterhood', in Centre for Contemporary Cultural Studies, *The Empire Strikes Back: Race and Racism in Seventies Britain*. London: Hutchinson, pp. 212–35.

Carter, C., Clegg, S.R. and Kornberger, M. (2008) *A Very Short, Fairly Interesting and Reasonably Cheap Book About Studying Strategy*, London: Sage.

Castells, M. (1996) *The Rise of the Network Society*, Massachusetts and Oxford: Blackwell.

Caygill, H. (2013) *On Resistance: A Philosophy of Defiance*, New York and London: Bloomsbury.

Clark, J. (1984) *The Anarchist Moment. Reflections on Culture, Nature and Power*, Montreal and Buffalo: Black Rose Books.

Combahee River Collective (1979) 'A Black Feminist Statement', [online] available from: http://circuitous.org/scraps/combahee.html [accessed 20 September 2019].

Crenshaw, K. (1989) 'Demarginalising the Intersection of Race and Sex: A Black Feminist Critique of Anti-discrimination Doctrine, Feminist Theory and Antiracist Politics', *University of Chicago Legal Forum*, 140: 139–67.

Day, R.J.F. (2005) *Gramsci is Dead. Anarchist Currents in the Newest Social Movements*, London and Ann Arbor: Pluto Press.

Dean, J. (2009) *Democracy and Other Neoliberal Fantasies: Communicative Capitalism and Left Politics*, Durham and London: Duke University Press.

De Geus, M. (1989) *Organisatietheorie in de Politieke Filosofie*, Delft: Eburon.

De Geus, M. (2014) 'Peter Kropotkin's Anarchist Vision of Organization', *ephemera: theory & politics in organization*, 14(4): 853–71.

della Porta, D. and Diani, M. (2006) *Social Movements. An Introduction* (2nd edn), Malden: Blackwell.

Díaz Nafría, J.M. and Al Hadithi, B.M. (2009) 'Are "the Semantic Aspects" actually "Irrelevant to the Engineering Problem"?', *tripleC*, 7(2): 300–8.

Dolgoff, S. (1989) *The Relevance of Anarchism to Modern Society*, Chicago: Charles H. Kerr.

Duda, J. (2012) 'The Idea of Self-Organization between Science and Politics', PhD thesis, The Johns Hopkins University.

Duda, J. (2013) 'Cybernetics, Anarchism and Self-Organisation', *Anarchist Studies*, 21(1): 52–72.

Dupuis-Déri, F. (2016) 'Is the State Part of the Matrix of Domination and Intersectionality? An Anarchist Inquiry', *Anarchist Studies*, 24(1): 36–61.

Dworkin, G. (1988) *The Theory and Practice of Autonomy*, Cambridge: Cambridge University Press.

Epstein, B. (2001) 'Anarchism and the Anti-Globalization Movement', *Monthly Review*, 53(4), [online] available from: http://monthlyreview. org/2001/09/01/anarchism-and-the-anti-globalization-movement/ [accessed 07 September 2019].

Escobar, A. (2009) 'Other Worlds Are (Already) Possible: Self-Organisation, Complexity, And Post-Capitalist Cultures', in J. Sen and P. Waterman (eds) *World Social Forum. Challenging Empires*, Montreal: Black Rose Books, pp. 393–404.

Espinosa, A. and Harnden, R. (2007) 'Complexity Management, Democracy and Social Consciousness: Challenges for an Evolutionary Learning Society', *Systemic Practice and Action Research*, 20(5): 401–12.

Espinosa, A., Harnden, R. and Walker, J. (2004) 'Cybernetics and Participation: From Theory to Practice', *Systemic Practice and Action Research*, 17(6): 573–89.

Espinosa, A., Harnden, R. and Walker, J. (2008) 'A Complexity Approach to Sustainability – Stafford Beer Revisited', *European Journal of Operational Research*, 187: 636–51.

Fiske, J. (2011) *Introduction to Communication Studies* (3rd edn), London and New York: Routledge.

Franks, B. (2003) 'The Direct Action Ethic from 59 Upwards', *Anarchist Studies*, 11(1): 13–41.

Franks, B. (2006) *Rebel Alliances. The Means and Ends of Contemporary British Anarchisms*. Edinburgh and Oakland: AK Press.

Freedman, L. (2013) *Strategy. A History*, Oxford: Oxford University Press.

Fuchs, C. (2012) 'Social Media, Riots, and Revolution', *Capital & Class*, 36(3): 383–91.

Fuchs, C. (2014) *Social Media. A Critical Introduction*, London: Sage.

Fuchs, C. and Sandoval, M. (2014) 'Introduction. Critique, Social Media and the Information Society in the Age of Capitalist Crisis', in C. Fuchs and M. Sandoval (eds) *Critique, Social Media and the Information Society*, New York and London: Routledge, pp. 1–47.

Galloway, A.R. (2014) 'The Cybernetic Hypothesis', *differences: A Journal of Feminist Cultural Studies*, 25(1): 107–31.

Gerbaudo, P. (2017) *The Mask and the Flag: Populism, Citizenism and Global Protest*, London: Hurst and Company.

Geronimo (2012) *Fire and Flames. A History of the German Autonomist Movement*, Oakland and Sunderland: PM Press.

Giraud, E. (2015) 'Subjectivity 2.0: Digital Technologies, Participatory Media and Communicative Capitalism', *Subjectivity*, 8(2): 124–46.

Goldman, E. ([1910] 1969) *Anarchism and Other Essays*, New York: Dover Publications.

Goldman, E. (1924) 'My Disillusionment in Russia', [online] available from: https://theanarchistlibrary.org/library/emma-goldman-my-disillusionment-in-russia [accessed 07 September 2019].

Goldman, E. (1940) 'The Individual, Society and the State', [online] available from: https://theanarchistlibrary.org/library/emma-goldman-the-individual-society-and-the-state [accessed 27 September 2019].

Goodman, P. (2010) *New Reformation: Notes of a Neolithic Conservative*. Oakland and Sunderland: PM Press.

Gordon, U. (2008) *Anarchy Alive. Anti-Authoritarian Politics from Practice to Theory*, London and Ann Arbor: Pluto Press.

Gordon, U. (2016) 'Democracy: The Patriotic Temptation', [online] available from: https://crimethinc.com/2016/05/26/democracy-the-patriotic-temptation [accessed 08 September 2019].

Gordon, U. (2017) 'Anarchism and Nationalism', in N. Jun (ed.) *The Brill Companion to Anarchism and Philosophy*, Leiden: Brill, pp. 196–215.

Gordon, U. (2018) 'Prefigurative Politics between Ethical Practice and Absent Promise', *Political Studies*, 66(2): 521–37.

Graeber, D. (2009) *Direct Action: An Ethnography*, Edinburgh and Oakland: AK Press.

Graeber, D. (2013) *The Democracy Project. A History. A Crisis. A Movement*, London: Allen Lane.

Graham, R. (2011) 'Colin Ward: Anarchy and Organisation', *Anarchist Studies*, 19(2): 84–91.

Gullestad, M. (1992) *The Art of Social Relations: Essays on Culture, Social Action and Everyday Life in Modern Norway*, Oslo: Scandinavian University Press.

Gunn, R. (2014) 'Yes, But', [online] available from: http://bellacaledonia.org.uk/2014/09/14/yes-but/ [accessed 20 September 2019].

Gunn, R., Smith, R.C. and Wilding, A. (2015) 'Assemblies for Democracy: A Theoretical Framework', [online] available from: http://assembliesfordemocracy.org/2015/07/14/assemblies-for-democracy-a-theoretical-framework-by-richard-gunn-r-c-smith-and-adrian-wilding/ [accessed 20 September 2019].

Hardt, M. and Negri, A. (2004) *Multitude. War and Democracy in the Age of Empire*, London: Penguin.

Harnden, R. (1989) 'Outside and Then: An Interpretive Approach to the VSM', in R. Espejo and R. Harnden (eds) *The Viable System Model. Interpretations and Applications of Stafford Beer's VSM*, London: John Wiley, pp. 383–404.

Hayles, N.K. (1999) *How We Became Posthuman. Virtual Bodies in Cybernetics, Literature, and Informatics*, Chicago and London: The University of Chicago Press.

Hill Collins, P. (2000) *Black Feminist Thought: Knowledge, Consciousness, and the Politics of Empowerment*, New York: Routledge.

Holloway, J. (2010) *Crack Capitalism*, London: Pluto.

Holloway, J. (2011) 'ZAPATISMO', [online] available from: www.johnholloway.com.mx/2011/07/30/zapatismo/ [accessed 07 September 2019].

Holloway, J. (2016) *In, Against, and Beyond Capitalism: The San Francisco Lectures*, Oakland and Sunderland: PM Press.

hooks, b. (1981) *Ain't I a Woman? Black Women and Feminism*, Boston: South End Press.

hooks, b. (2000) *Feminism is for Everybody. Passionate Politics*, Cambridge: South End Press.

hooks, b. and Lowens, R. (2011) 'How do you Practice Intersectionalism? An Interview with bell hooks', [online] available from: http://blackrosefed.org/intersectionalism-bell-hooks-interview/ [accessed 20 September 2019].

Jaggar, A. (1985) *Feminist Politics and Human Nature*, Totowa: Rowman and Allanheld.

Jarrett, K. (2008) 'Interactivity is Evil! A Critical Investigation of Web 2.0', *First Monday*, 13(3).

Jensen, K.B. and Helles, R. (2011) 'The Internet as a Cultural Forum: Implications for Research', *New Media & Society*, 13(4): 517–33.

Jeppesen, S., Kruzynski, A., Lakoff, A. and Sarrasin, R. (2014) 'Grassroots Autonomous Media Practices: A Diversity of Tactics', *Journal of Media Practice*, 15(1): 21–38.

Jones, G. (2018) *The Shock Doctrine of the Left*, London: Polity.

Juris, J.S. (2005) 'The New Digital Media and Activist Networking within Anti-Corporate Globalization Movements', *Annals of the American Academy of Political and Social Science*, 597: 189–208.

Juris, J. (2008) *Networking Futures. The Movements Against Corporate Globalization*, Durham and London: Duke University Press.

Juris, J. (2012) 'Reflections on #Occupy Everything. Social Media, Public Space, and Emerging Logics of Aggregation', *American Ethnologist*, 39(2): 259–79.

Katsiaficas, G. (2001) 'The Necessity of Autonomy', *New Political Science*, 23(4): 547–55.

Katsiaficas, G. (2006) *The Subversion of Politics. European Autonomous Social Movements and the Decolonization of Everyday Life*, Edinburgh and Oakland: AK Press.

Khatib, K., Killjoy, M. and McGuire, M. (2012) *We are Many: Reflections on Movement Strategy from Occupation to Liberation*, Edinburgh and Oakland: AK Press.

Kinna, R. (2005) *Anarchism: A Beginner's Guide*, Oxford: Oneworld.

Kinna, R. (2019) *The Government of No One. The Theory and Practice of Anarchism*, London: Penguin.

Kinna, R. and Prichard, P. (2019) 'Anarchism and Non-Domination', *Journal of Political Ideologies*, 24(3): 221–40.

Kinna, R., Prichard, P. and Swann, T. (2019) 'Occupy and the Constitution of Anarchy', *Global Constitutionalism*, 8(2): 357–90.

Kline, R. (2015) *The Cybernetic Moment. Or Why We Call Our Age the Information Age*, Baltimore: Johns Hopkins University Press.

Kokkinidis, G. (2014) 'Spaces of Possibilities: Workers' Self-Management in Greece', *Organization*, 22(6): 847–71.

Kropotkin, P. (1898) 'Anarchism: Its Philosophy and Ideal', [online] available from: https://theanarchistlibrary.org/library/petr-kropotkin-anarchism-its-philosophy-and-ideal [accessed 25 July 2020].

Kropotkin, P. (1910) 'Anarchism', [online] available from: http://theanarchistlibrary.org/library/petr-kropotkin-anarchism-from-the-encyclopaedia-britannica [accessed 08 September 2019].

Kropotkin, P. (1927) *Kropotkin's Revolutionary Pamphlets* (R.N. Baldwin (ed.)), New York: Vanguard Press.

Landemore, H. (2015) 'Inclusive Constitution-Making: The Icelandic Experiment', *Journal of Political Philosophy*, 23(2): 166–91.

Lazar, H. (2015) 'Until All Are Free. Black Feminism, Anarchism, and Interlocking Oppression', [online] available from: https://anarchiststudies.org/until-all-are-free-black-feminism-anarchism-and-interlocking-oppression-by-hillary-lazar/ [accessed 20 September 2019].

Leach, D.K. (2009) 'An Elusive "We". Antidogmatism, Democratic Practice, and the Contradictory Identity of the German Autonomen', *American Behavioral Scientist*, 52(7): 1042–68.

Leach, D.K. and Haunss, S. (2008) 'Scenes and Social Movements', in H. Johnston (ed.) *Culture, Social Movements, and Protest*, Farnham and Burlington: Ashgate Publishing, pp. 255–76.

Leonard, A. (1996) 'Team Syntegrity: A New Methodology for Group Work', *European Management Journal*, 14(4): 407–13.

Leonard, A. (2013) 'Viable Systems Model Revisited. A Conversation with Dr Allenna Leonard', *The Systematic Excellence Group*.

Lievrouw, L. (2011) *Alternative and Activist New Media*, Cambridge: Polity.

London Edinburgh Weekend Return Group (1979) 'In and Against the State', [online] available from: https://libcom.org/library/against-state-1979 [accessed 09 April 2020].

Lorea (n.d.) 'Welcome to Lorea.org', *Lorea*.

Lovink, G. (2011) *Networks Without a Cause. A Critique of Social Media*, Cambridge and Malden: Polity.

Luhmann, N. (1995) *Social Systems*. Stanford: Stanford University Press.

Lundström, M. (2020) 'Towards Anarchy: A Historical Sketch of the Anarchism-Democracy Divide', *Theory in Action*, 13(1).

Maeckelbergh, M. (2009) *The Will of the Many: How the Alterglobalisation Movement is Changing the Face of Democracy*, London: Pluto Press.

Maeckelbergh M. (2012) 'Horizontal Democracy Now: From Alterglobalization to Occupation', *Interface*, 4(1): 207–34.

Maeckelbergh M. (2014) 'Social movements and global governance', in M. Parker, G. Cheney, V. Fournier, C. Land (eds) *The Routledge Companion to Alternative Organisation*, London: Routledge, pp. 345–58.

Mandiberg, M. (ed.) (2012) *The Social Media Reader*, New York: NYU Press.

Mason, P. (2011) *Why It's Kicking Off Everywhere. The New Global Revolutions*, London and New York: Verso.

Maturana, H. and Varela. F. (1980) *Autopoiesis and Cognition: The Realization of the Living*, Boston: Reidel.

McEwan, J.D. ([1963] 1987) 'Anarchism and the Cybernetics of Self–organising Systems', in C. Ward (ed.) *A Decade of Anarchy (1961–1970). Selections from the Monthly Journal* Anarchy, London: Freedom Press.

McQuail, D. (2010) *McQuail's Mass Communication Theory*, London: Sage.

Mead, M. (1968) 'Cybernetics of Cybernetics', in H. von Foerster (ed.) *Purposive Systems. Proceedings of the First Annual Symposium of the American Society for Cybernetics*, New York and Washington: Spartan Books, pp. 1–11.

Medina, E. (2011) *Cybernetics Revolutionaries. Technology and Politics in Allende's Chile*, Cambridge: MIT Press.

Milburn, K. (2019) *Generation Left*, London: Polity.

Mill, J.S. (1977) *On Liberty*, New York: Penguin Books.

Milstein, C. (2010) 'Democracy is Direct', [online] available from: https://revolutionbythebook.akpress.org/ak-tactical-media/pamphlet-no-2/ [accessed 27 September 2019].

Moore, J. (2004) *I Am Not a Man, I Am Dynamite! Friedrich Nietzsche and the Anarchist Tradition*, New York: Autonomedia.

Morozov, E. (2011) *The Net Delusion. How Not to Liberate the World*, London: Allen Lane.

Mueller. T. (2003) 'Empowering Anarchy. Power, Hegemony, and Anarchist Strategy', *Anarchist Studies*, 11(2): 122–49.

Nunes, M. (2010) 'Error, Noise, and Potential: The Outside of Purpose', in M. Nunes (ed.) *Error: Glitch, Noise, and Jam in New Media Cultures*, New York: Continuum International Publishing, pp. 3–23.

Ólafsson, J. (2016) 'The Constituent Assembly: A Study in Failure', in V. Ingimundarson, P. Urqualino and I. Erlingsdóttir (eds) *Iceland's Financial Crisis. The Politics of Blame, Protest and Reconstruction*, London: Routledge, pp. 252–72.

O'Reilly, T. (2005) 'What Is Web 2.0?', [online] available from: http://oreilly.com/web2/archive/what-is-web-20.html [accessed 20 September 2019].

Pangaro, P. (1996) 'Cybernetics and Conversation', [online] available from: www.pangaro.com/published/cyb-and-con.html [accessed 10 September 2019].

Pask, G. ([1961] 1968) *An Approach to Cybernetics*, London: Hutchinson.

Pask, G. (1976) *Conversation Theory. Applications in Education and Epistemology*, Amsterdam, Oxford and New York: Elsevier.

Pickerill, J. and Chatterton, P. (2006) 'Notes Towards Autonomous Geographies: Creation, Resistance and Self-Management as Survival Tactics', *Progress in Human Geography*, 30(6): 740–6.

Pickering, A. (2010) *The Cybernetic Brain. Sketches of Another Future*, Chicago and London: University of Chicago Press.

Plato (1997) 'Alcibiades', in J.M. Cooper and D.S. Hutchinson (eds) *Plato. Complete Works*, Cambridge: Hackett, pp. 557–95.

Price, W. (2007) 'What is Class Struggle Anarchism?', [online] available from: https://theanarchistlibrary.org/library/wayne-price-what-is-class-struggle-anarchism [accessed 20 September 2019].

Prichard, A. (2012) 'Anarchy, Anarchism and International Relations', in R. Kinna (ed.) *The Continuum Companion to Anarchism*, London and New York: Continuum, pp. 96–108.

Proudhon, P.-J. (1840) *What Is Property? An Inquiry into the Principle of Right and of Government*, [online] available from: https://theanarchistlibrary.org/library/pierre-joseph-proudhon-what-is-property-an-inquiry-into-the-principle-of-right-and-of-governmen [accessed 20 September 2019].

Rauch, J. (2014) 'Exploring the Alternative-Mainstream Dialectic: What "Alternative Media" Means to a Hybrid Audience', *Communication, Culture & Critique*, 8, doi: 10.1111/cccr.12068.

Resnick, M. (1996) 'Beyond the Centralized Mindset', *Journal of the Learning Sciences*, 5(1): 1–22.

Resnyansky, L. (2014) 'Social Media, Disaster Studies and Human Communication', *IEEE Technology and Society Magazine*, Spring: 54–65.

Rheingold, H. (2003) *Smart Mobs: The Next Social Revolution*, Cambridge: Perseus.

Rowbotham, S. (1979) 'The Women's Movement and Organizing for Socialism', in S. Rowbotham, L. Segal and H. Wainwright (eds) *Beyond the Fragments: Feminism and the Making of Socialism*, London: Merlin Press, pp. 21–55.

Ruesch, J. (1957) 'Principles of Human Communication', *Dialectica*, 11(1): 154–66.

Ruesch, J. and Bateson, G. (1968) *Communication. The Social Matrix of Psychiatry* (2nd edn), New York: W.W. Norton & Company.

Sandoval, M. and Fuchs, C. (2010) 'Towards a Critical Theory of Alternative Media', *Telematics and Informatics*, 27: 141–50.

Savran, Y. (2016) 'The Rojava Revolution and British Solidarity', *Anarchist Studies*, 24(1): 7–12.

Scott, B. (2004) 'Second-Order Cybernetics: An Historical Introduction', *Kybernetes*, 33(9/10): 1365–78.

Seeds for Change (2013) 'A Consensus Handbook', [online] available from: www.seedsforchange.org.uk/handbookweb.pdf [accessed 8 September 2019].

Seeds for Change and Anarchy Rules (2018) 'Anarchic Agreements', [online] available from: www.seedsforchange.org.uk/anarchic_agreements.pdf [accessed 27 September 2019].

Shannon, C.E. (1949) 'Communication in the Presence of Noise', *Proceedings of the I.R.E.*, (January): 10–21.

Shannon, C.E. and Weaver, W. (1949) *The Mathematical Theory of Communication*, Champaign: University of Illinois Press.

Shannon, D. and Rogue, J. (2009) 'Refusing to Wait: Anarchism and Intersectionality', [online] available from: https://theanarchistlibrary. org/library/deric-shannon-and-j-rogue-refusing-to-wait-anarchism-and-intersectionality [accessed 20 September 2019].

Shantz, J. (2010) *Constructive Anarchy. Building Infrastructures of Resistance*, Farnham and Burlington: Ashgate.

Simmel, G. (1971) *On Individuality and Social Forms*, Chicago and London: University of Chicago Press.

Sitrin, M. and Azzellini, D. (2014) *They Can't Represent Us! Reinventing Democracy from Greece to Occupy*, London: Verso.

Stirner, M. (1995) *The Ego and Its Own*, Cambridge: Cambridge University Press.

Swann, T. and Ghelfi, A. (2019) 'Pink Organising: Notes on Communication, Self-Organisation, Noise and Radical Social Movements', *Organization*, 26(5): 696–715.

Swann, T. and Husted, E. (2017) 'Undermining Anarchy: Facebook's Influence on Anarchist Principles of Organization in Occupy Wall Street', *The Information Society*, 33(4): 192–204.

Tero, A. et al. (2010) 'Rules for Biologically Inspired Adaptive Network Design', *Science*, 327: 439–42.

Terranova, T. (2000) 'Free Labour: Producing Culture for the Digital Economy', *Social Text*, 18(2): 33–58.

Terranova, T. (2012) 'Attention, Economy and the Brain', *Culture Machine*, 13(1): 1–19.

Tilly, C. (2010) *Regimes and Repertoires*, Chicago: University of Chicago Press.

Truscello, M. and Gordon, U. (2013) 'Whose Streets? Anarchism, Technology and the Petromodern State', *Anarchist Studies*, 21(1): 9–27.

Ulrich, W. (1981) 'A Critique of Pure Cybernetic Reason: The Chilean Experience with Cybernetics', *Journal of Applies Systems Analysis*, 8: 33–59.

Umpleby, S. (1987) 'ASC Glossary on Cybernetics and Systems Theory', [online] available from: ftp://ftp.vub.ac.be/pub/projects/Principia_Cybernetica/Nodes/Cybernetics_glossary.txt [accessed 27 September 2019].

Van de Sande, M. (2013) 'The Prefigurative Politics of Tahrir Square – An Alternative Perspective on the 2011 Revolutions', *Res Publica*, 19(3): 223–39.

Van de Sande, M. (2015) 'Fighting with Tools: Prefiguration and Radical Politics in the Twenty-First Century', *Rethinking Marxism: A Journal of Economics, Culture and Society*, 27(2): 177–94.

Van Duyn, R. (1972) *Message of a Wise Kabouter*, London: Duckworth.

Volcano, A. and Rogue, J. (2012) 'Insurrections at the Intersections. Feminism, Intersectionality and Anarchism', [online] available from: https://theanarchistlibrary.org/library/abbey-volcano-j-rogue-insurrections-at-the-intersections [accessed 20 September 2019].

Von Clausewitz, C. [1832] 1997) *On War*, Ware: Wordsworth.

von Foerster, H. ([1960] 2003) 'On Self-Organizing Systems and Their Environments', in H. von Foerster (ed.) *Understanding Understanding. Essays on Cybernetics and Cognition*, New York: Springer, pp. 1–19.

von Foerster, H. ([1991] 2003) 'Ethics and Second-Order Cybernetics', in H. von Foerster (ed.) *Understanding Understanding. Essays on Cybernetics and Cognition*, New York: Springer, pp. 287–304.

von Glasersfeld, E. (1991) 'Editor's Introduction', in E. von Glasersfeld (ed.) *Radical Constructivism in Mathematics Education*, Dordrecht: Kluwer, pp. xiii–xx.

Walker, J. (2001) 'The Viable Systems Model: A Guide for Co-operatives and Federations', [online] available from: www.esrad.org.uk/resources/vsmg_2.2/pdf/vsmg_2_2.pdf [accessed 14 July 2020].

Walter, W.G. (1963) 'The Development and Significance of Cybernetics', *Anarchy*, 25: 75–89.

Waltz, M. (2005) *Alternative and Activist Media*, Edinburgh: Edinburgh University Press.

Ward, C. (1966) 'Anarchism as a Theory of Organization', [online] available from: http://theanarchistlibrary.org/library/colin-ward-anarchism-as-a-theory-of-organization [Accessed 07 September 2019].

Ward, C. (1973) *Anarchy in Action*, London: George Allen and Unwin Ltd.

Weaver, W. ([1949] 1973) 'The Mathematics of Communication', in C.D. Mortensen (ed.) *Basic Readings in Communication Theory*, New York: Harper and Row, pp. 27–38.

Wiener, N. (1961) *Cybernetics; or Control and Communication in the Animal and the Machine* (2nd edn), New York and London: MIT Press and John Wiley & Sons.

Wilson, M. (2014) *Rules Without Rulers. The Possibilities and Limits of Anarchism*, Hants: Zero Books.

Yassin-Kassab, R. and Al-Shami, L. (2018) *Burning Country. Syrians in Revolution and War*, London: Pluto.

Yates, L. (2014) 'Rethinking Prefiguration: Alternatives, Micropolitics and Goals in Social Movements', *Social Movement Studies*, 14(1): 1–21.

Index